-A Success Story-

FROM CLUTTER
To Cleanliness:

The Renewal Of A Mind

True Ju

True Ju Enterprises

TRUE JU

From Clutter To Cleanliness: The Renewal Of A Mind

- A Success Story

Disclaimer - The information presented in the chapter "What To Say, And How Not To Say It" (So you don't say what you're not supposed to say) is original, but in no way conclusive. However, great effort has been taken to ensure that the reader understands the concepts presented, and that new Statements of Desire can be correctly spoken and successfully implemented into your daily life. By the time you are done reading this chapter, you will absolutely know how to form and speak your own Statements of Desire, empowering your life forever more.

First edition

ISBN: 979-8-9865736-4-9

Editing by True Ju Enterprises
Cover art by True Ju Enterprises
Agent: True Ju Enterprises

This book was professionally typeset on Reedsy.
Find out more at reedsy.com

For Little Jujee; the strongest boy I've ever known. My hero.

Contents

Foreword

"BE OF STRONG WILL EVEN WHEN NOBODY HAS DONE IT BEFORE" -
It takes a strong will power for one to bring his vision to manifestation. You have to be intelligent, organized, courageous even when nobody has ever done it before you.

If you work consistently and constructively, the world has no choice but to let you through and eventually give you your own niche.
-Chukwuemeka Chidi

————————————————

From Clutter To Cleanliness: The Renewal Of A Mind - A Success Story, will guide you into the subject matter of self-healing, learning how to identify your intuition, self-empowerment, uncovering some of the most effective affirmation techniques, and many other methods the author has adopted into his life since arriving to earth.

The aspect of this book that sticks out the most is quite possibly the perspective from which all of this life-altering information is viewed from. The author shares his personal experience, one which is so far from the typical allure and grandeur of the so-called New Age community, that it offers us a rare look into a world-view that many people don't often experience. This particular world-view is constructed in such a way that those who are blessed with their own experiential world-view outside of the one shared in this book wouldn't be keen to articulate it from a basis of personal experience. In other words: every link found on the chain of life is intrinsically connected.

Then, there are a group of individuals whom have the experiential world-view described in this book, but don't have the mentality or desire to articulate the experience, which eventually leads to a non-documented moment in physical space that will never be extrapolated upon or made available to be carefully dissected and studied for future enlightenment.

If this book was a gift that you would've never thought to purchase yourself, and you've read this far but have already began to doubt the validity of the content, or even told yourself "none of this describes me so far...why should I keep reading?", then this book is in the hands of the one that it is definitely supposed to be in, and I highly suggest you continue reading it!!!

From Clutter To Cleanliness: The Renewal Of A Mind - A Success Story will have you reading with anticipation and excitement each time you pick it up. It is filled with anecdotes prescribed by so-called "Urban communities", capturing a certain flavor not typically seen in a work of this magnitude.

The author provides you with a real-time, successfully implemented approach to living in the 21st century, along with tips covering a vast range of knowledge kept away and hidden from the masses, or "Gen-Pop", another term for the masses referred to in this book.

It is advised that you relax, clear your mind, and keep an open heart regarding the different concepts you will read within these pages. Although some of the concepts and ideas presented may be entirely new to you, or initially make you feel uncomfortable, nothing presented here is meant to hurt or confuse you.

Each and every one of us get to experience our own unique journey, with that uniqueness binding us into collectivity. It is our pursuit towards inner-growth that resonates with people all across the world. There's always a goal set, a mark achieved, and a long-standing record broken. Just like there's always some new goal being set in order to distinguish one member of society from another.

The honest truth is: this earth and who we are as humans is one huge performance stage where we are all serving as the living camera system for the Creatoress/Creator of this universe. Now if you simply take a moment to trust the intuition within, the voice that carried you to this place and time, continuing to read, you will see how all of this, and more, applies to you; right now.

A WORD: The Kingdom of God

"Very truly I tell you, no one can see the kingdom of God unless they are born again."

I finally get it: unless you change your thinking, aka become "born again", you'll always believe the Kingdom of God is OUTSIDE OF YOU; renew your mind aka change your thinking, and you will find, and KNOW, that the Kingdom of God within YOU!

Science has proven that what we see 👀 begins inside of US, then we see it OUTSIDE of ourselves as the images our brains register.

This is why it is so important to CHANGE our thinking, and focus on the Kingdom to come; leave this wicked kingdom alone: we have a doper one on the way.

Imagine, once all who are meant to see the Kingdom, see it within first, THEN, what is seen from within by many, will MANIFEST itself outside of all those who looked within….that is why the Kingdom of God will appear and be seen in A BLINK OF AN EYE!!!

"Neither shall they say look there or look here, for the Kingdom of Heaven is within you!" - Luke 17:21

In other words: the Kingdom of God WILL NOT APPEAR until we Children of God aka the little Gods and Goddesses, beginning with the Lost Sheep, innerstand this great Key.

Once the Chosen ones COLLECTIVELY AWAKEN to this truth…it's GAME OVER.

ACTION: Go to the downtrodden, the poor, and the street people…share this great news with them, that we hold within us the Keys To Heaven, and that we've been Redeemed as Children of The Most God, back to Itself so that the Word, who became flesh, might be realized and honored within us all! - Asé

-True Ju§

From Clutter To Cleanliness: The Renewal Of A Mind
-A Success Story

Preface

- *"Believe It You Will Achieve It"*

———————————————

In society today there is much to be said concerning social influence and its ability to manipulate an individual's psyche into being persuaded in a manner antithetical to ones natural inclinations. The majority of the time, those societal ills are perpetuated outside of the home. Unfortunately however, they are oftentimes propagated within the home. The outside, always finding a way to creep and slither in.

The realities of peer-pressure are not just felt during primary and general schooling, but throughout life. We all, in one way or another, experience the intoxicating spirit of peer-pressure and find its effects difficult to shake if given over to its whims.

"Peer-pressure" is oftentimes formed in the invisible realm of thought.

The widely accepted view on peer-pressure is that it takes shape in the mind of someone who seeks to do something or have some-thing done, which others are uncomfortable with. Sometimes it's a thing someone may be uncomfortable with themselves, or that someone is sought after to do, that others are comfortable with, but it's always conveyed in an awkwardly uncomfortable, hurtful, confused, or destructive manner, all of which usually end with disastrous results.

At its proverbial and energetically charged root, peer-pressure can motivate a person to greatness or motivate them into mediocrity; the challenge is identifying whose pressure will inspire you to greatness and whose pressure will motivate you into mediocrity.

What or who is authentic? What or who is keeping it real? Are those who we esteem to have these attributes of "realness" worthy of our attention or following? In this New Millennium, the answers to these questions are often fleeting or perplexingly difficult to identify and grasp.

These questions take on an entirely new meaning in the age of verifiable social media accounts, and influencer's who've never signed one autograph or responded to one fan letter, but have millions of people tune into their lives daily. Whatever these influencers say or do seems to eventually become "law", at least until a new influencer comes along later and changes the commonly held belief or popularly accepted narrative. It's rather ironic that an individual, as well as the information or knowledge of an individual, won't be considered valid unless backed by corporate approval, especially when the individual isn't given say in how the corporation operates on a daily basis.

Maybe we should also begin asking the question "who verifies the verifier?".

This might seem random, but I remember a time when "Old wives tales" were the go-to source for an alternative thought concerning anything embarrassingly private, secretive, or taboo; you know, all of the "uncomfortable to openly speak about" type of stuff. Often claimed to be unverifiable stories passed down from generation to generation, it's quite amazing that an idea finding its original inspiration within the depths of the imagination could make its way onto the physical plane, and endure the tests of time. Someone had to have experienced a small taste of some kind of actual life-changing event, which then found its way into cultural lore.

Not swimming "for at least an hour after eating", not crossing your eyes or "they'll get stuck that way", and my personal favorite: drinking the flavorful soda Mountain Dew will kill your sperm cells (although consuming soda and large amounts of caffeine and yellow dye 5 will negatively impact fertility), are some old wives tales that have continued to proliferate within the national cultural landscape.

So many people are looking for the answers to questions they've asked themselves over and over again, not realizing the answer they seek is held deep within. Being verified and being validated are two different things. When we begin to trust ourselves, we at the same time begin to validate ourselves.

Take a moment to imagine a world where everyone has the confidence, the pressure within, to push themselves into the greatness they've always imagined obtaining. These people wouldn't need external validation to be who they've always wanted to become, and no one would be able to sway their personal convictions away from how they've envisioned themselves to be.

The thoughts and concepts expressed in this book are the culmination of many years of intimate observation, purposeful filtration, and honest application.

The purpose of this book is to assist you in realizing that you aren't alone in what you're facing day to day. It was written so that you might grasp meaningful concepts and formulas that will assist you in renewing your mind. If you were led to this book, be it given to you as a gift, purchased from online, or won in a raffle, you were supposed to receive it.

You will encounter many confirmatory statements as you read these pages.

Please do your best to embrace what you read, and do not feel threatened with the illusory idea that someone who thinks like you, has also done something you feel *you're* supposed to do but haven't done yet, so mental frustration creeps in causing you to doubt the path etched out for you. Look at this book as one huge confirmation that you are exactly where you are supposed to be in life, that your righteous ideas and inspirations are worthy of pursuit, and will one day be shared with the world!

-True Jus

From Clutter To Cleanliness: The Renewal Of A Mind
  -A Success Story

1

"I Was Raised In The Slums"

I'm not gon' tell it all. Just enough.

It's almost funny when I think about it. The famous cliche, used to help one identify their upward trajectory through life's social caste system. The media uses it all the time. Athletes all over the world use it. From professional Basketball's Number One pick, to professional Boxing's next Champion, heck, even professional Tennis has found a way to identify its next generation of Rising Stars as somehow "coming from the slums"; a true rags-to-riches story. The famous cliche, used to fuel one into the stratosphere of success, providing them reason to work hard, an excuse to be callous, and the determination to "never look back". The problem is, that when we use this cliche, we are always looking back. Yes, we are always looking back, and oftentimes, we are looking back with resentment, anger, and bitterness.

Resentment, anger, and bitterness are the ingredients which fuel this trajectory, and somebody, someone "out there somewhere" knows this, and has been using this storyline to encapsulate millions of avid fans and supporters to invest time and money into yet another young, promising athlete, musician, scientist, doctor, or future media mogul, and honestly, it would seem that modern society, no matter how far along we advance, has a complete fixation on the narrative that has given justification to the resentment, anger, and bitterness that many of the most successful people in today's landscape have harnessed to fuel themselves into the very success they are being celebrated for. These individuals rise through the ranks of their respective industries, receive recognition, become financially rich beyond their wildest dreams, with many even becoming iconic, but in all of this success and achievement, where is the healing?

Could this be the reason why so many reach the pinnacle of their lives, attaining all they've ever wanted, but are still unhappy? Is this the reason why many successful people fill utterly empty inside, and hopeless once they've reached the highest levels of success?

Well, I was raised in the slums too. However, I was so embarrassed about where I was raised that I would never dream of sharing my upbringing with the world. The types of people I sought to be around, and the types of rooms I'd dreamed of being invited into would never tolerate such a vagabond; such a social outcast. It's not that I didn't "have a home", it's just that the home I had held so many secrets; so many reasons as to why I couldn't talk about "where I was from". I was almost always feeling inadequate and unwilling to share the rawest and realest aspects of my life, because the adults who were commissioned to take care of me, would probably get in trouble, or at the very least, be embarrassed about what I revealed to the world in order to meet the narrative ideology of "I was raised in the slums". See, I had always sought to protect the adults in my life from utter embarrassment and chastisement from their peers, but the truth is, they were suppose to feel a sense of higher responsibility towards me, and were the ones who were suppose to protect me from embarrassment and chastisement from *my* peers.

I was born at Alta Bates Hospital on July 2, 1985 in Berkeley, California at approximately 5:20 a.m.. It was a Tuesday. A beautiful, golden Tuesday. It was warm, with a slight, occasional breeze. The day seemed promising. Up to that point, my mother had done her best to make sure my journey into this realm was free of hardship, struggle, and pain. I was her first child after all. A new mother-to-be is usually a ball of emotion, happy one moment, nervous another, and anxious the next. Unsure about how well her first full-term pregnancy will go, hoping for the best, but never quite settling into that surety, which is supposed to confirm to her that everything will indeed be okay. I was originally supposed to be born on the Fourth of July. Something happened though, which would change my due-date, pushing it up two days, and confirming to my mother that everything actually might not be okay; at least up to that point in her pregnancy with me.

A day before what would become my actual birth-date, my mother went to the local grocery store because she had a serious craving for some watermelon. My family is pretty big on eating watermelon; it's a cultural thing. Her father, my maternal-grandfather Julius, was always picking and purchasing the absolute finest watermelons you could imagine from local growers who'd sell the fruit in stands along the side of the road; he was a true expert at identifying the juiciest, most succulent watermelons; a gift he would eventually pass on to me. The growers he chose to patron were organic farmers before "organic" was even a thing; it's just how regular people grew produce back then, especially those who wanted to earn a living farming but had a limited budget. On this particular day however, it was not my grandfather who would provide his daughter, my mother, with the watermelon she had been craving, so she went to the store to purchase one. Back in the 1980's, it wasn't to uncommon to enter into a fruits and vegetables section of the store with the realization that the food had been sprayed with some sort of insecticide. The insecticide used was usually a form of a harmful substance known as DDT, and the purchaser was never made aware of just how much of the damaging toxin was actually used at any given time. Even though the insecticide had been banned and dwindling in use, it's very difficult for farmers, even the farmers of today, to make an immediate switch to regulated farming practices that the government implements. So, when my mother purchased what she thought was a healthy, juicy watermelon, it turned out that what she had actually purchased was in fact a toxic, fruitfully looking time bomb.

When my mother consumed the watermelon, she thought little to nothing about its future affects on her body, and mine. As her body began to digest the watermelon, she grew very ill. She told my dad that something didn't seem to feel right, and that the baby, me, was not happy. Once my dad got them both safely to the hospital, she began going into labor with me. It was at this moment that something was clearly wrong. The doctors asked her what she ate and she told them. Based off of her symptoms, they felt that she'd possibly been poisoned by bad fruit. She was immediately induced for cesarean section. I was removed from my mother's womb, a ten pound baby boy, but I was unable to breath on my own. The reason I could not breath on my own is because the poisonous watermelon turned my mother's amniotic fluid into a thick syrup-like substance. That substance, mixed with the bile I had produced while in her womb, had somehow found its way into my lungs, making me unable to successfully take those first critical breaths of air.

We were separated. The chest-to-chest bonding time that a new mother usually has with her new child did not take place. Instead, I was rushed to the neonatal intensive care unit, or NICU, where I'd spend the first of my earliest days on this earth, being tended to by nurses whom had never quite seen a baby going through what I was experiencing. This was my mother's first real heartbreak. Truth be told it was my first heartbreak as well. This would also prove to be the first attempt by the Enemy to take me out of the Game of Life early, but my angels, as well as the Most High Mama & Papa, my Heavenly and Divine Parents, had a different idea about that. Unfortunately, or fortunately, depending on how you look at the glass, either being half full, or half empty, this wouldn't be the last time that the Enemy tried its hand at taking me out.

During my early toddler-hood, in the month of February 1986, my mom, who was working a full-time job at the University of Berkeley, and my dad, enjoying his freedom after retiring from police work with Oakland Police Department, had been keeping me at a neighbors apartment during the daytime to be babysat. My babysitters were a cool young couple who hadn't had children yet, but they had toys, and they were into cats. I've always loved cats, I really think it's an ancestral thing, and toys well, they were beginning to grow on me a little.

One day, February 8, 1986, while inside their apartment, it's said that I began playing with the toys as I normally did, and that I placed some of them into my mouth to control the swelling from my new set of teeth that were growing in. The teething must have been so immense, that by the time my babysitters realized what I was doing, I had already gone minutes into using the toys as teething rings. The following series of events would alter my existence for the next fifteen years, and would prove to be the second attempt by the Enemy on my still very young life.

On February 9, 1986, I had become quite uncomfortable and had developed a strong fever, well over 102 degrees, as well as a strawberry-colored and textured rash on my tongue. By February 10, 1986 my parents decided to rush me to Oakland's Children's Hospital at the behest of my pediatrician. A medical team met us at the hospital upon entry and rushed me to a unit for immediate treatment. In order to break my temperature and avoid testicular sterilization, I was placed into a tub of ice. This practice isn't implemented any longer, but at the time, it was what doctors thought was best to lower a body temperature back to normal conditions.

The experience was quite traumatic for both of my parents and it was the first time that my mom saw my dad cry.

I remained in the hospital under close supervision until February 19, 1986. During my stay, I was diagnosed with a rare condition called Kawasaki Syndrome, a "condition that causes inflammation in the walls of some blood vessels in the body, which is most common in infants and young children." It is still recognized as a very mysterious ailment, which doctors believe is brought on by something external to the body. Once I was finally released, I had to continue visiting Oakland's Children's Hospital annually for fifteen long years so that doctors could study and record its full-blown effects. I was the "only Black boy in the entire Bay Area" that had the syndrome, and due to it's potential to induce debilitating damage to the heart muscle, it was suggested that I be seen and tested by a veteran cardiologist to determine its proper function throughout my childhood into my becoming a teenager. What this all meant to me and my desire for physical activities was that I could not participate in any strenuous sports. Football, Basketball, and Soccer were all sports I dearly wanted to play, but was unable to participate in, at least until the age of fifteen. Martial arts, and Baseball were the sports selected for me to participate in, and in which I excelled. However, during those early days I always held a sense of bitterness because I felt limited and truly believed I was physically fit to play any sport I desired to play. I also had to wear a bulky, Walkman-like device called an EKG Reader, which had sticky-pads which were strategically placed over areas of my chest to record my heart's vitality and activity. The results from each reading would be recorded at Oakland's Children's Hospital, and would assist the cardiologist in making the eventual determination that I was healthy enough to participate in the sports I'd always wanted to play. Although I was indeed grateful to finally be considered healthy and cleared by my cardiologist to play strenuous sports, the aspect of this realization for my parents was that they'd grown comfortable with me not playing any sport where weekend involvement and travel was required. Plus, I had missed out on NJB (National Junior Basketball) and Pop Warner, so by the time I was a sophomore in high school, none of the coaches new who I was or had any familiarity with my talent level. I didn't know at that time the importance of parents, especially my dad, vouching on my behalf to the coaches so that I could be highly considered to play on their teams. I don't think my parents realized this either, but there was honestly very little effort on their part to even find out.

Entering into my teenage years was rough on me. I did not feel properly equipped. Subconsciously comparing what I had to what the other children had was a constant inner-battle that I did my best to ignore. Sometimes "the battle" was brought right to me no matter what I did to avoid the ills of being a teenager forced to live in such a fast-paced, materialistic world. "Like Mike,

I wanna be like Mike" was a successful brand campaign jingle made famous by the basketball superstar Michael Jordan. I raised in an era where Michael Jordan was that guy everyone still wanted to be like. It seemed like children, especially little boys, had the best and most valid chance at being "like Mike" and oh did we try. If you weren't a star on someone's basketball team, couldn't shoot the ball well, or couldn't slam dunk the ball ferociously through the hoop, the only option left was find someone who would purchase you the shoes; yes, those shoes.

The Jordan Brand line of footwear became the most successful shoe-line that Nike ever released. Children all over America, especially us in the inner-cities, had to have a pair. They were a cultural phenomenon. People would ditch school just to line up for hours so that they might be lucky enough to purchase a pair of J's, as we call them. If you couldn't make it to the shoe store in time to locate your size, perhaps there would be someone willing to sell you a pair at an increased price. Even if the seller wore the shoes one time, the value they retained was still worth the hassle, and definitely well-worth the cool points one would earn upon arriving to school with the hottest kicks in the whole world on their feet. This era was also extremely brutal. The Jordan Brand of shoes was incredibly high-priced. There were certain children, many children actually, whose parents were unable to afford such a high-priced shoe. Due to the popularity of the shoes, with so many children unable to afford them, they became a target for thieves, robbers, and eventually even killers. Yes, many people lost their lives because they were fortunate enough to afford a pair of Jordan shoes, but unfortunate enough to have the wisdom to relinquish those shoes when confronted by violent thieves who sought to take them. As the shoes increased in production and popularity, so did the body count of those unfortunate ones who died trying to protect their parents investment. All throughout Junior High and High school, I can remember individuals placing their new shoes into their designated lockers before P.E. class was to begin, and returning to those lockers, pried open, with book bags sprawled across the locker room floor, shoes missing, with no indication as to who the culprit was. This happened often, but people kept on buying those shoes!

I would garner a sense of empathy for all of those who had their shoes stolen, but honestly, it was in those moments that I was most happy no one was interested in my "K-Mart Kickers". In some strange, twisted way, I'm sure I was often looked at the culprit in such occasions because I was one of the "have-nots". One of the children who could not afford to purchase Jordan's, and I was always friends or associated with the children from the same geographical placements as me, so who better than to orchestrate an elaborate scheme of thievery than me!? What always freed me from suspicion however, is that I usually only had one pair of shoes at any given time, so if I was the culprit, I sure did have a funny way of not wearing the shoes I desperately needed after allegedly being the one who had stolen them! Plus, how could I earn "cool points" by *not* wearing the shoes I'd allegedly stolen? What was I doing, only wearing them on the weekends and non-student days? Lol

Life works out in funny ways. It's flow is unmatched by even the fiercest rivers and streams. What makes us laugh can, and will, make us cry. What's good for you, doesn't have to be good for me. What's bad for you, can be good for me. What's bad for us both can just be, well, bad; until someone comes along that finds goodness in that supposed bad thing. It's all perspective based. These perspectives are what add variance and a certain spice to life. Understanding this simple principle is surely one of the key reasons I've been able to finally accept my childhood, early home environment, and all of the lessons learned from those seasons of my life.

I still love me some watermelon too.

2

"Clutter. Hoarding. Squalor."

"The moment when you want to quit is the moment you need to keep pushin'"
-Kush and Wizdom

We didn't always live in a hoarder-house.

Something happened.

Something happened that changed our living conditions for quite a long time, that none of us understood. We did our best to deal with it at first, but over time, as the conditions worsened, it was obvious that living like this for much longer was simply not going to work in the best interests of everyone living within the four walls of this blessed, but damaged-looking home. Fixing and remediating our dear Aunt Sallie and Uncle Sid's home back to the glory it once held wasn't going to be an easy task. How did our home get like this? How did we get to this point?

When we lived in Alameda, CA our apartment was always clean. A normal, two-bedroom, upper-level unit that was well furnished with plenty of space for a young family of four. Our kitchen was always clean, and the cabinets

9

usually held many canned goods, pots and pans, as well as a few household supplies, just like any other home that I'd been in up to that time. As a little child, I didn't even know hoarder-homes existed.

During this season of my life, one of my older brothers came to live with us. He was my dads youngest son, from his previous marriage. I loved when my big brother Tim, affectionately known as Teeter, came to stay with us. Our parents made room for him, and he moved right in. He was a young, growing teenager at the time, who desperately needed to make contact with our father. I'm still grateful to this day, that our dad obliged him, and allowed him to make his journey to California from Chicago a reality. Oakland and Chicago had long been considered Sister-Cities, especially during the Civil Rights movement, and advent of the Black Panther Party. Alameda is about 4 minutes from West-Oakland, the birthplace of the Oakland Chapter of the Black Panther Party, and home to one of its founders and public face of the organization, Huey P. Newton.

Life had always felt good to me during the eighties. I was born in the middle of the decade. The second half of the eighties was filled with innovation in the technology industry. My generation was the last to fully experience both analog, and digital technologies at the same time. We were in a unique position as the newest babies and children on earth, at a time when the promise of global technology was being propagated without a sure idea on how it would actually look or take effect on a global scale. When my brother arrived, life actually got better for me. One thing about my dad that I always loved, was that he told me about my siblings from his previous marriage early on in my life; I'd always known I wasn't his oldest, or first-born child, but that I was my moms first-born child. What I didn't know however, is that it would eventually be revealed, many decades into the future, that I was one of nineteen children that my father sired, and that I had a sister, three months older than me, living in West-Oakland, four minutes away from where we lived. More on that later.

During the late eighties, and into the nineties, my mother, little brother, and I, would often travel to South Richmond to visit our dear Uncle Eddie. He loved our company and we loved his. He had a clean, well furnished home, that was suitable for a widower of his age. My aunt Lillian, his one and only wife, had passed away before I was born, so I never got to meet her in person, only hearing about her occasionally. My uncle did have a housekeeper who was older in age, but younger than him named Elise, who happened to live down the street. She would come and tend to him on a regular basis, and was working for him by the time I was born. She also ended up taking a lot of money from him, while in cahoots with my mom's younger sisters husband, during the final year of Uncle Eddie's life. Who would've thought?

Teeter had a great time staying with us for a few years. Time flew by, he finished high school and then went back to Chicago. By 1989, our dad had decided that he wanted to go into business for himself after completing a lengthy law-enforcement career. He established his private security company that year, and still operates it to this very day. Uncle Eddie, was nearing the end of his long journey here on earth, and decided that it was time to start preparing for his exit. In the 1970's, when his wife Lillian passed away, he decided to purchase two grave plots, one for her, and one for him, located right next to hers. He was also the beneficiary of many assets, one of which he gifted to my mother, his favorite niece. What he decided to gift to my mother, was his elder sister Sallies home, located in Vallejo, CA, that he'd been overseeing, ever since Aunt Sallie and Uncle Sid had passed away. This gifted home, would allow my parents to stop paying rent, and assist my dad financially so that he could build up capital to further establish his private security services. Uncle Eddie loved my mother dearly, and by extension, he loved anyone connected to her. He was also a visionary of sorts, so when he caught wind that my dad was starting a business, Uncle Eddie wanted him to be as successful as possible, even if only for our sake. My parents decided to leave Alameda for Vallejo in 1989, during the climax of the crack epidemic. When we arrived, the neighborhood that Aunt Sallie and Uncle Sid were familiar with was no more; if they would've still been alive, there is

11

no doubt they would've been heartbroken at what was transpiring in a once affluent neighborhood.

The city of Vallejo was actually still quite segregated at that time. There were only a few Indigenous ("Black") neighborhoods in the city, ours being one of them. It was kind of tricky to navigate because of the city's attachment to the United States Navy. The Mare Island naval military base was the first naval installation on the west coast. Submarines were manufactured there, along with nuclear weapons and energy; it was a real military destination in its heyday, with many enlisted soldiers and officers making it their home. The government created special housing units off-base, which were designed specifically for high-ranking officers and their families. There weren't many, if any, Indigenous ("Black") military officers during those days, so the majority of those special homes were erected with European descent ("White") occupancy in mind. All of the enlisted soldiers were housed in project buildings located in the inner-city, forcing them to travel to the military base daily, as opposed to being housed on or near the base.

There was a Denny's restaurant located on the waterfront in Vallejo, that was a "Whites Only" establishment, which all of the military families would patron well into the late eighties and early nineties. I still remember my maternal grandfather joyously talking mess to the folks his age who would look at us crazy when we finally got to eat at that restaurant as a family; he would literally crack me up with laughter because everyone his age knew exactly why he felt the way he did. Times were still tense in many places of the nation, but we would navigate through them together, so the sting of racism wasn't felt by us children as much. Technology also played a key role in the systematic removal of overt racism, an effect we didn't realize was taking place within society at first.

Back at home in our neighborhood, the crack epidemic was reaching its climax; I'm talking about real "Night of The Living Dead" type stuff was taking place. We had a bus line that ran right in front of our home on Springs

Road, that was relocated to Florida street, behind Churches Chicken, because people kept getting robbed as they waited for the bus. The scourge of criminal activity was growing daily, and my people were truly lost mentally, physically and spiritually. The one thing that saved us from being totally destroyed is that we still had many of our old-timers alive and with us, who were doing the best they could to keep their children and grandchildren on the straight and narrow, even though the temptation of this new drug was running rampant everywhere, not just in Vallejo.

The year was 1990 when my mom got pregnant with her third child. My younger brother Justin and I, we're pretty excited to have a new sibling. This was back in the early nineties, so I don't know if gender reveal technology was available yet. Some years later I'd learn that if a woman is carrying low, she is more than likely having a boy, and if she is carrying high that she is more than likely carrying a girl. I do remember my mom's tummy being rather large though. One day she asked my brother and I to bet on what we felt she was going to give birth to. Whoever won the bet would get a double-scoop ice cream cone from Thrifty's. I think we both bet we were having a baby brother, so no ice cream cones for either one of us! The pregnancy seemed to be typical. No issues or complications were experienced by my mother, but I do remember taking that final stretch to activate her maternity leave from work at the University, and begin preparing herself mentally to give birth to her third child. Her elder brother Keith, and his wife Aurora, or "Ro" for short, were major factors in our lives at that time, and would always come over to our house while we stayed in Alameda. We'd also take the quick drive over to their house in Oakland. They and my parents would always go on double-dates, frequently having cool nights out on the town. Once we moved to Vallejo, they kept the energy high, and would make the drive to come and see us, never coming empty-handed. My Auntie Ro always kept a freezer bag full of cough drops and she would give Justin and I a handful a piece, and sometimes more if we'd ask for them; we'd eat them things like gobstoppers, just crunching away!

The adults would get together after dinner, set up the card table, and begin playing their favorite card game "High-Low". My brother and I would be off to the side playing with our toys, or doing something creative while also eat hustling, or peeking at them play the game in an attempt to learn it for ourselves. Even though we had just moved to Vallejo, and hadn't quite settled in, the house was for the most part orderly and clean on the inside, with a few boxes of belongings that still needed to be placed wherever they were intended to go, but, if I may, nothing was "out of the ordinary". The memory of the home originally belonging to moms grand-aunt Sallie still reverberated inside of her with scenes from her childhood playing in her mind. My mom walked very carefully in that house when we first arrived as if Aunt Sallie still lived there; in a sense she did, and I know I could feel her presence for sure, even though I never had the chance to meet her in this particular cycle of life. Aunt Sallie was a strong, respected woman. Not manly strong, but mentally strong. She was well respected because she stood up for women at a time when others wouldn't, and she still maintained the respect she commanded for her husband Sid. She was very balanced in her approach to women's issue and femininity. She also owned a United States patent for her hair pomade formula that she sold to her clients. To this day, my mom swears that the hair product "Sulfur8" is our Aunt Sallies formula repackaged. If anyone would know, my mom would because she was Aunt Sallie's little apprentice, mixing and stirring the formula for hours to get the consistency right, before it would eventually be packaged for sell.

My brother and I were attending the one and only private school we'd experience in life, during our moms third pregnancy. It was a Christian-based school named Noah's Ark, and was actually the school where I had originally met Desanté for the first time; we were placed into the same kindergarten class together. I remember my mom beginning to show her first signs of frustration with me around the latter moments of her pregnancy. I think that the move to Vallejo, not finishing the unpacking process, getting us into school for the first time, doing her best to help my brother and I with our homework, and not feeling the sense of total assistance from my dad, really began to take its toll on her mentally, physically, and spiritually. Also, during this time, dad would still travel back and forth from Vallejo to Alameda and Oakland. He would eventually invite his friend Ellis Thomas, also known as E.T., to live with us, which I think would have to be the beginning of all of the additional discord and disfunction that we would begin experiencing as a family. I'm still not sure on how he and E.T. met, but I do remember he and E.T. hanging out back in Alameda. Once we moved to Vallejo, they wanted to maintain their friendship. E.T. had been married and even had two children, a daughter and a son, but he and his wife ended their marriage; perhaps that's what pushed him into alcoholism. He was a Choctaw Indigenous man, who definitely embodied the old adage that one should "never give an Indian alcohol to drink." He loved combing his hair back and holding it down with Murray's hair pomade and warm water. He'd place a wave cap, also known as a durag, over his head, and allow it to set before removing it from off of his head. Sometimes he'd keep it on for the duration of the day, just like we've all been guilty of doing at one point or another. E.T. loved wearing his "cowboy" boots, as my brother and I called them, and he was an aspiring musician who owned a beautiful black electric blues guitar. He loved smoking squares, also known as cigarettes by most, and he would let me play his guitar often. He was a cool guy over all, and I'm sure that's why my dad liked having him around. The issue only seemed to arise when my dad would pay more attention to he and E.T.'s escapades than to the attention my mom needed and desired, especially as her third pregnancy grew more intense. By the time my mom was ready to give birth, E.T. was given my brother and I's bedroom to sleep in and we were moved to the living room floor to sleep during bedtime. "Floor-time" might be the more appropriate term though.

It was January the 22nd, the middle of winter, when my little sister was finally born, and she entered into this physical realm with a bang, literally. My mom could've never predicted what was going to eventually transpire during her delivery. She had always been a focused and driven mother, keeping up with doctors appointments and making sure she watched her diet, eating the best foods her pregnancy would allow her to. During the time she carried my sister, she had a desire to eat salads and fruits, and a variety of soups. She didn't eat too much seafood, if any, and she stayed away from heavy meats like beef and pork.

Leading up to my sister's due-date, my mom kept up with her doctors appointments and had already decided on an OG-GYN. The doctor she chose was supposed to be on-call around the agreed upon date that my mom would be going into labor. Instead of making himself available on the day my sister was to be born, he decided to go to Tahoe on a skiing excursion because they had received a record snowfall. My mom was naturally upset, but was forced to go with the flow in order to keep the vibe positive. She was assigned a new OB-GYN when her and my dad got to the hospital. This new obstetrician was not familiar with my mother's birthing plans. According to mom, the obstetrician didn't even want to be at work that evening. Before driving to the hospital, my mom called Uncle Keith for some assistance. She asked if he could meet us at the hospital to get my brother and I, so that we could stay at his house while our sister was being born. He quickly drove over to Alta Bates, and met us in the hallway of my moms delivery room. Once we left the hospital, my uncle made a quick detour to the grocery store to purchase some fresh milk and a box of cereal for breakfast. My brother and I loved going to Uncle Keith and Auntie Ro's house. He was an avid San Francisco 49ers fan and had a lot of cool sports memorabilia that we loved looking at. He also had our favorite film Moonwalker, by Michael Jackson, and kept a full bowl of M&M's on the coffee table. Whatever was going to transpire at the hospital, we wouldn't be worried or thinking about it because we'd be occupied and enjoying ourselves at Unc's house. We watched the movie as best we could because it was really late in the evening. Once we finally fell asleep it was early in the a.m..

We awoke to a couple bowls of Kellogg's Nut & Honey Crunch and a phone call from the hospital. Uncle Keith seemed a little frazzled. He didn't have children, but he took care of us like we were his own. He also was a medic during his service in the United States Army; he knew a thing or two concerning the sensitivity of delivering medically related bad news. While my brother and I were eating cereal, Uncle Keith informed us that something happened to our mom at the hospital, and that we'd have to stay with him a little while longer. We found out we had a new baby sister, so excitedly we were expecting to see her and our parents.

When we finally got to the hospital, our mom was still energetically drained for delivering our sister, but she was also in excruciating pain. What happened to her over the course of the evening while giving birth would alter our lives forever.

After a little due-diligence and a lot of ear hustling, Justin and I found out that our mother had been terribly injured during the birthing process. We found out that she had a C-Section, and that during the moments of her womb being opened, her bed collapsed. This freak accident caused an injury to her spinal column that would take decades to heal. At the same time the bed collapsed, the nurses realized that the umbilical cord, meant to provide my sister oxygen, was actually wrapped multiple times around her neck. This near fatal occurrence caused my sister to turn purple with oxygen deprivation. The nurses had to move swiftly if they were to save her life. In a rush to remove my sister from our mother's womb, and untangle the umbilical cord, they immediately closed my moms womb. However, they were rushing so quickly that they closed it incorrectly. Mom would later find out that her womb had been sewn to her abdomen, causing her additional pain. The entire ordeal caused great internal damage and was the source of deep depression for my mom.

Uncle Eddie's health also took a turn for the worse. My mom was unable to tend to him as he'd expected she was supposed to, and this made him sad during the final years of his life. My mom blamed herself for not being able to see him as frequently as she had before her injury. In 1992 on his birthday, Uncle Eddie passed away. I was just about to turn seven. I missed my uncle and I missed the great energy my mom used to have. Times were about to get rough. This was also the official beginning of the household full of clutter, that would eventually lead to my mom hoarding, which ultimately would cause the squalor we'd be forced to live in for quite some time.

When I was a child I was more embarrassed than angry. I always knew that if my mom could control her depression, we definitely wouldn't be living the way we were. The frustration came whenever we, my dad, brother and I, attempted to clean the house. Most of the purchases my mom made in the years to come would primarily be from estate sales, thrift stores, and liquidation sales. She had pretty good taste, and she is a very nostalgic woman. You see, whenever my mom purchased something, she would see the value in it, regardless of the era it came from. She expected us to see the same value in it. She was also purchasing many of these items to release the stress of depression she felt from not being able to go back to work in her career at the University. I guess her goal was to purchase these items wholesale, and sell them at a later date. She always loved the idea of yard sales, but every time she got around to it, her back would flare up, causing her tone bed-ridden and moan in pain. Seeing her cry because her body hurt so badly made me not complain about the house growing more disorganized and disorderly by the day. My dad couldn't do much because he wasn't a doctor, and didn't want to be. He also didn't do much because he figured she'd eventually heal and finally sell all of the items she'd acquired in the years after her injury. The injury also caused great emotional strife between the two of them because their sex-life was affected. Even though they'd go on to have one more child together, my baby brother Joseph would be the last between them. I often wondered what would've happened if my dad had shown a little tenderness and sensitivity to my mom, instead of focusing on his security business and hanging with his friends outside. In my opinion, the "hanging with the guys" was a leading issue to my moms sustained depression because she often wondered if she was still seen as a valued asset in my dads eyes. Whenever she had a "good day" health wise, she use it by making even more purchases that we simply didn't need in the house. I will say this: if "if" was a fifth, we'd all be drunk!

I was embarrassed because I knew what the inside of my home looked like. I couldn't have any friends from school come over to my house ever. That meant no sleep-overs on the weekend, and no board games or video games played inside my home. If I was to kick it with any of my friends from school, I'd have to visit their home. I'm super grateful to my friends and their parents who were understanding and allowed me to visit them. I was also embarrassed because I never had a place that motivated me to complete my school work. My grades sunk tremendously from the second grade, all the way up to high school. Somehow I'd be promoted to the next grade to continue school. My teachers knew I was a bright child. Perhaps they also knew that there was more I was facing daily than what met the eye. I'm grateful to them as well for never prying into my home life, and placing added pressure on me to tell a story I wasn't ready to narrate yet.

I attended Highland Elementary school from the first grade through the sixth grade. During those early years I made the Honor Roll one time, which was during the fourth grade. My teacher at the time, Mrs. Tomek, really enjoyed me. She showed it every day and she gently expected greatness from me, similarly to how my mother did from ages 1-5. Mrs. Tomek actually recommended that I be placed into the GATE Program for academically gifted children, but when it was time for me to take the test I purposely bombed it because I didn't want to leave Highland and all of my friends. Plus, I knew the truth taking place at home: how was I going to attend a gifted school across town when I didn't have the necessary tools at home to compete and stay motivated in an environment that required my absolute focus? I walked to school everyday because my dad didn't like getting up too early to take us to school. I walked home every day because he'd be too busy by the afternoon to pick us up. How was this potential new schooling arrangement actually going to work? By this time, my attending the "gifted school" was just going to add a false sense of glimmer to my parents lives that none of us actually needed. I felt like I'd go from "all E's" (equivalent to "A's") in the fourth grade to all "N's" (equivalent to "F's") by the time I received my first report card from the gifted school because of this. I completed the eighth grade and was promoted to the ninth grade from Springstown Middle School, formerly known as Springstown Junior High School. My ninth grade freshman year at Vallejo High was like taking a stint in California Youth Authorities or juvenile hall; it was really a trip. If I wasn't from the Hood, I would've gotten eaten alive. Many children lost their way during those informative years. I'm grateful to still be here to tell my story.

During the years of my mom's depression and slow healing, she joined the PTA board, and also attended School Board meetings. During these meetings she'd vouch for children all over the city, demanding we have greater resources at our disposal. She'd vouch for children she didn't even know. While at home, her own children didn't have adequate studying amenities to help us focus on completing assignments. We didn't have to worry about "the dog eating our homework" because if we'd sat a paper down for even five minutes, it might get lost in the piles of "important papers" my mom would keep for her own important records and references database. Life was tough but each of us children found ways to cope with what was going on. I'm thankful I never turned to alcoholism or drugs during those years. I just did my best. I never spoke about my condition, keeping these secrets to myself well into adulthood.

The beginning of the summer of 2000 changed our family dynamics profoundly. My mom and dad had a reached a true emotional crossroads in their marriage. Arguments increased daily. My dad was becoming frustrated with the condition of the house. My mom was growing more and more comfortable with its condition. Something was going to give, or something was going to be taken. My dad decided to get CPS involved. I think he was under the delusion that they would immediately take his side. Whenever you get the authorities involved, you can rest assured that they will shake everything up to suit their own agenda, and that's exactly what happened. In order to get proof of our living conditions, my dad asked me to take photographs of each room. I was frustrated with our home's conditions too, so I foolishly followed his instructions and took the pictures, unaware of the consequences that would follow. As a father myself now, I wouldn't have asked one of my children to do that task. The future strain, that one decision I made in obedience to my dad, created between my mom and I, has lasted into my adulthood, and she has never saw me in the same light. It is up to her to forgive me, but it is also up to her and my dad to recognize there own hands in the conditions that festered within our home, causing that moment to manifest. She still hasn't been able to admit that things got out of line because of her inability to cope with her depression in a healthy manner. My dad still hasn't been able to hold himself accountable for not being emotionally available to my mom, and if you were to ask him how the house got to the condition it was in, he'd say his wife, my mom, was the reason. Even though they've never sought my forgiveness, I have forgiven them many times.

What I worry about most is whether or not they will recognize the discord and dysfunction their actions caused our family. Without an honest examination of what took place between them, I'm afraid they will continue to sweep the past under the rug, never truly healing from the emotional turmoil, which will cause their hearts to remain heavy. We must learn how to keep it real with each other, even when the truth is uncomfortable. Keeping it real assists us in easing the karma and lightening the emotional load placed into the deepest recesses of our consciousness. In this way, we can identify harmful traits within ourselves and correct them before they fester and propagate into subsequent generations.

Once CPS got involved and saw those images I snapped, they immediately removed my siblings and I from our home. We had a meeting with the CPS agent in charge of our case. She interviewed me and each of my siblings individually. I coached my siblings so that our replies to the CPS would give us the best chance of not being separated and placed into group homes. We all answered her questions and were placed together at my Auntie Elaine's home for the remainder of the summer. We were just grateful we weren't separated, even though we were confused about what the rest of our lives would look like. CPS ordered my mom to clean up the house before we were to return. I had to leave with a small bag of underwear, my toothbrush, and a couple items of clothing.

I never made it back home to Aunt Sallies house.

When I finally snuck back inside the home one day while my mom was away, I had outgrown everything that I was forced to leave behind in my drawers. The house was still in horrible condition, and I felt like Peter Pan in the film *Hook*, returning to the Tree Trunk in Neverland for the first time since becoming an adult. Seeing the house remain the same, if not worse, made me feel like my mom didn't want me to come back. It was difficult because my emotional attachment to the home was still strong, and I wanted her to live up to her side of the bargain struck with CPS; to clean the house so that her children would be able to return home.

My dad ended up getting an apartment up the street and around the corner from Aunt Sallies. I stayed with him for the remainder of high school, which at that time was the tenth through twelfth grades. We kept the apartment clean, and I was able to start having a couple of my friends come over. I was still bitter for not being able to return home, but I was also beginning to get used to what life could be like for me if I lived in a home that was consistently cleaned, organized, and had space for me to stretch out in.

Throughout my time at VHS, I was often placed into the worse and most disorderly classes, oftentimes not having a teacher for months, and sometimes for an entire school year. We'd be forced to sit in the school auditorium until a suitable substitute teacher was located. I missed out on a lot of valuable information. Many of my peers from that era dropped out. I realized later in life that I dropped out too, I just didn't have anywhere to go during those hours, and with no money or anything to eat, I just attended school for the "free" breakfasts and lunch.

When the moment finally arrived in June of 2003, I graduated by the one or two hairs on my chin at the time, with a 1.68 gpa from Vallejo High School. At least I graduated; THANK YOU Most High Mama & Papa! It felt surreal to walk that line. I didn't know what I was going to do with my life at that point so I joined the Marine Corp, and was placed into their Delayed Entry program because I was seventeen and hadn't graduated yet. Once I received my diploma and began walking off the football field with my peers, I was met at the exit gate by two Marine Corp corporals looking to take me to get processed at MEPS, to get sent on a flight to Camp Pendleton to begin Basic Training. Wow.

I ended up not going to Basic Training. I got out of the Marine Corps with a letter from the Northern CA Commander stating that I was "unfit for duty" and that I wouldn't be required to participate in a draft should their be one due to a that heart condition I previously told you about from my childhood. My recruiting officer had me lie on my application to join the service, and when the Corp found out about my smudged paperwork right before I was to fly down to Camp Pendleton, they kicked my booty up out of their system quickly! They didn't want me being "collateral damage". I don't blame em. I didn't know what I was going to be doing with my life at this point, but I kept the faith that something magnificent was in store for me.

I told you earlier that I'm not looking for any pity, or to express myself as being a victim in all of this. At least I had a home. At least I had two parents living their with me. At least I had the fortitude to deal with these issues in the highest frequency possible. At least my heart never got cold. Upon some deep inner-reflection, I have much to be grateful for; believe it or not, it could've been a lot worse. Being an early July baby, I would often find it difficult to let go of the past, especially those moments where I felt disrespected, let down, or not cared for.

I had to learn that letting go of a painful past gets easier when we look at it as "they were just doing what they had to do, everything that was cosmically necessary, for us to find the light in ourselves." They weren't thinking like that obviously, but on a soul development level that is exactly what was happening. Shout out to brother Josh Roberson for sharing that insight with me.

You see, I wouldn't be the man I am today if I hadn't gone through those moments. I also wouldn't look at life the way I do now had I chosen a different approach to coping with those moments while I was living through them.

Once I was free and clear from my enlistment into the military, I took a deeper look at my abilities to write and produce music. Before I initially began writing, I had to ask myself a couple of questions. "What makes you feel like you can even do this?", and "why would anybody listen to you; what do you have to say about anything?"

The answers to my questions were simple. "I'm from a place that all these "Rap cats" wanted to be from. I have a real story to tell. I'm not going to be lying in my lyrics to fake the funk; I'm truly from it." That was my answer to myself. I stood on them.

One day, I met this studio and record-label owner who gave me my first studio gig. It wasn't what I expected but I appreciated it for what it was. He was converting his "outdated" analog equipment into a digital workspace, and he was going to be selling the analog equipment, so he needed help unplugging and taking everything apart so it could be boxed up and sold. He was also working on a television show deal he had in place for a major television network in the Bay Area. What he needed was a theme-song written for his new show and asked me if I would write it and record it. I was asked to do that job in exchange for recording time concerning my own project, in a real studio, as well as the recording being turned into a pressed up single for distribution. I didn't know about all of the business jargon involved, but I was getting closer to my dream being fulfilled, so I agreed.

The record label office and recording studio was very cool. It was comprised of an entire upper-floor of a building on Tuolumne street I'd walked by a thousand times on my way home from school, but never knew until then what was inside. I immediately realized that I loved this job and that this is what I wanted to do for as long as I could.

Time fly's when you're having fun, and it was no different there. Three hours seemed to go by in thirty minutes. I couldn't get enough of the place. After I successfully took down, labeled, and boxed up all of the audio connectors and cords, I began work on the theme-song for his show. I still didn't know how to record myself, especially on his production equipment that he decided he'd be keeping in the studio, so he had to show me. Once I learned how to run things, he left me alone with the instrumental of the theme-song playing so that I could get into my song-writing groove.

Up to this point, I had been writing lyrics, whole songs, since sixteen years old. I was now nineteen years old, and feeling like I was finally touching my dream. As I was writing in the studio, sitting on the black leather couch, he would keep checking on me, making a bunch of distracting statements that I had to do my best to ignore if I was going to successfully write his show's theme-song. Writing that theme-song meant that I could then begin recording my single. Just as I was finally getting into my writing groove, he called me into his office. I told him "hold on, give me a minute" and then made my way to his office which was next to the recording studio room.

As I made my way to his office, I took full notice of a green-screen, camcorder, and a tripod that had been setup in a lounge area right in front of his office. I had noticed it before as I walked into the studio to begin working, but I wasn't trying to look all around and "snoop", so I kept my tunnel vision and just walked into the lab. It wasn't until I was asked inside of his office that my attention turned to the recording camera and green-screen setup.

I walked into his office and he offered me a seat to sit down. His desk had a lot of papers on it. There was a picture inside of a frame that was faced away from me. He turned it around so I could see it. Who I saw in the picture blew my mind. It was a picture of Eminem, aka Marshall Mathers, sitting in his office, right here in Vallejo, looking into the camera like "yo what up, it's Eminem." He told me "yeah, Eminem came through, he comes to the Bay often, he's definitely been to Vallejo as you see. We were working on something." I was like "whaaaaat, I'm sitting in an office that Eminem sat in?" My mind was blown. He then wiggled the mouse to his computer to get it off of screensaver mode so he could show me elements to his distribution network.

I was impressed, but I could only see what he wanted to show me though. I took notice of that. It was all an attempt to butter me up so that I'd sign a contract that he then presented to me. Before I had the chance to actually look at the contract, he asked me if I'd noticed the camera and green-screen. I said yes, and he told me that he filmed most of his show's opening sequences right there. His show's opening sequence featured him driving around in a flying microphone car to distant lands, while he was rapping the theme-song that I was to write. The sequence didn't have any sound elements added to it yet, so it was all visual. After watching that opening sequence, I was honestly ready to get back to writing. I had a clearer idea of what I wanted to write and I needed to get it down on paper. However, it was at this moment that he felt the need to show me one more thing. He disconnected the camera from the tripod and walked over to me with it. It was one of those cameras with the foldable and rotating screen, so once he adjusted it to where we could both see the image feed, he said "hey man, check this out."

At this point, I didn't know what he was going to show me. He hit the play button, and all of sudden I heard moaning and saw a young woman giving it up to some dude inside a dimly lit room. I initially thought I was watching a porno, until I realized the "dude" was him, and the dimly lit room was the recording studio where I'd been writing for the last thirty minutes. All I could do was think "oh man, what in the world..."

He was super juiced to be showing me this footage that I didn't ask to see or even know existed until that moment. As the tape ran, he would speed it up and then slow it back down. I grew pretty uncomfortable with what he was showing me. Every time I attempted to look away or change the subject, he'd excitedly roll more footage. He had at least six young women on this tape, at different times, performing a range of sex acts on him. He told me they all wanted recording deals and were going to have "to work" for them. I just looked at him. In my mind I was like "oh hell naw", but I really just wanted to punch him in the jaw for extorting those beautiful young women who had only sought to attain their dream of making music professionally just like I had.

He was essentially propositioning these young women to sign recording contracts in exchange for sex acts. If they were uncomfortable with the deals they signed later down the line and threatened to sue him, he'd blackmail them with the footage and force them to rethink any legal actions they'd want to make against him. Public humiliation is a real thing, and many unscrupulous people use this tactic to get what they want. This was the murky music industry that I had been warned about staring me straight in the face.

I also began thinking about how I met this dude in the first place. My mom is the one who introduced me to him. She had been working on his taxes and had been helping he and an elder woman with some litigation for a legal dispute they had with the city about some real estate properties. By this time, I realized that this dude was a certified scum bag, and I honestly couldn't help but wonder if this fool had gotten together with my mom, and had her on some footage too. I sure hoped not, but I could see the type of angles he played.

He turned the footage off and we walked back into his office. He had a huge grin on his face, and I was still just looking at him in slight disbelief of what I'd just been shown. I did my best to mask my disappointment. As the subject of the conversation turned back to the distribution element of the business, he handed me the five-page contract again. I took the contract that afternoon and looked it over, not aware of what I was actually signing. I told myself "as

27

long as I wasn't doing anything strange for a little (or big) piece of change, or selling my Soul, I guess this contract ain't bad." All I could think about once I reviewed the contract (still unaware of what I was reviewing) was that this was my first real opportunity to "make it" in the industry.

The traumatic experiences we face in life up to a certain point play a huge role in many of the decisions we make, and the crudest music and film executives know this about up and coming recording artists, actors, and actresses and use it as leverage against us. The desire I had to finish the project and get my single pressed up outweighed the hope I had that this guy and my mom didn't connect, that there weren't any other victims, and that he might have footage on them if they did connect.

I took the contract home. I signed the contract.

I didn't sell my Soul, but doing business, even in a small capacity with this guy, is definitely something I wouldn't engage in at this stage of my life. What did happen is that shortly after signing the contract, I began learning music industry law and I realized after rereading the contract that this dude would "own the rights to my stage name" for a number of years, essentially keeping me from working under that name. I left the dude alone for good once I completely understood what I had signed, and had to create a new name for myself so that I could continue recording independently. That is when "Skrippcha" was born.

I began writing lyrics like crazy, and I began producing my own sound through the beats that I'd create. I would book studio sessions in different people's bedroom studio's. After a while of doing this, always recognizing that I would dedicate more time to my sound if I had my own music production equipment, I began to look into purchasing my own gear. I knew I was going to need a computer, some speakers, a microphone and mic stand, some headphones, a popper-stopper, and some software programs so that I could produce and record my music. It was soon time to begin investing into my craft. If I was going to do this, it was going to be me, by myself, conducting the physical work, and my Angels and Ancestral Guides covering me from the Spiritual side of things.

When they say "pull yourself up by your bootstraps", which means to improve your position by your own efforts; that's exactly what I was doing. No complaints, but I often wondered who was in a higher position to actually assist me, just watching me, to see how'd far I would actually take my pursuits before giving up and quitting. I knew if I was going to achieve my goals I couldn't be thinking too long on these things though. I had to be about "dat action" or wasn't nothing going to get done. I knew I was talented, and this was still an era where an A&R could potentially scout you for a record deal. I was under the slight illusion that my talent would be discovered while I was performing a showcase at some bar & grill by an A&R looking for new talent. That someone would hear about me and pay me a visit, making me an offer to perform at "Freestyle Friday" on BET's hit show 106 & Park.

The people who I knew about, who were in those "higher" positions to help me, never came through. It was for the best too. I wasn't aware of the ills of the music industry when I first started out. I didn't know that Soul Selling was a real thing and that many of the people I thought I'd need to be in league with, were already gone, in league with the Devil, and they could see the Light within me. My Light scared off many demons and workers of wickedness that would've only had ill intentions for me, had my Spiritual guard been lowered. I say these things in hindsight, but while I was actively seeking someone else approval, it'd frustrate me that it seemed like I was getting nowhere in my music pursuits. In order to raise some funds I did a lot of odd-end jobs, doing my best to stay out of trouble.

One day I was told about a refinery shutdown-turnaround and potential job openings. A refinery shutdown-turnaround is basically the shutdown of an oil refinery, updating the maintenance and repair of it, and then restarting all of its systems for operation. I was told that a lot of brothers were making good, quick cash, and then able to leave the job and invest into what they really wanted to do, so I said "ok, Ima look into that." I was willing to do anything that would keep me free, and from doing anything strange to make a little change.

I took my first job out of high school at a chemical cleaning company and worked there for a few months. Twelve hour shifts, 6-7 days a week. Sometimes I'd work overtime and even double-time when the opportunity presented itself. I was initially happy that I had received the job, even though, like many others in this life, it wasn't what I actually wanted to do. As I worked hard, doing the tasks that the veteran employees no longer wanted to do, I'd be promised pay raises and opportunities to travel to sister locations in other states to increase my income. I'd work all hours, and in all types of weather conditions trying to "prove myself" to people who acted like they appreciated me and my working acumen, but secretly didn't.

I asked management about my promised pay raises frequently, especially when I found out other guys were placed into position to make more income but I was continually being looked over. Everything came to a head one day while I was hooking up a generator and chemical cleaning hoses to begin cleaning out a Coker at the refinery. I overheard one of the supervisors "joking" about "how much the equipment made per hour". The equipment that I was in charge of hauling from the yard, connecting, and operating successfully, was making about $180-$200 an hour. If the equipment was to be needed longer than a regular 12-hour shift, it would make overtime, and then if operations lasted beyond that, it'd make double-time. So you mean to tell me I'm working as hard as I'm working, never receiving a raise in pay, but this equipment, which wouldn't even be running and operating correctly if I wasn't watching over it, makes more than I do in a day, in one hour? Naw. No bueno. I put what would be my final request for a pay raise into management and was denied again. I worked a good one to two more weeks then I quit, I wasn't appreciated or being payed fairly, and they weren't going to be using me up.

I took my checks and cashed them. I didn't have a back account at the time, I went where every respected, hard-working individual went to cash their checks: the local La Tapatia market around the corner from Vallejo High School. Once I got my cash, I drove to the Concord CA Guitar Center and purchased what would be the first of many pieces of music gear and equipment. I felt accomplished. When I got all my gear back to my room at my dads place, I realized that I was going to have to learn how to actually use all of the stuff I just purchased. The learning curve was immense. I had purchased my first computer from a guy who refurbished them and installed them with larger RAM. When I began connecting all of the music equipment to the computer, and installed the music production software, I was ready to rock and roll. The recording software was a program called Cakewalk that was anything but a cakewalk to actually use. I wasn't feeling my vocal when I'd record myself and I knew that this wasn't the sound quality I was looking for, or had been used to from other studios. I had to figure out what I was doing wrong, and fast, or I'd be discouraged.

After everything I'd been through in my life up to that moment, I realized that recording music was my therapy. The microphone was my psychiatrist and the finished song was my healing. I literally needed to record and make music; it was my only genuine release.

At the time, I didn't realize that I was going to be creating my own lane within the music industry landscape. I didn't know that I'd be protected from making a crucial mistake within it. I didn't know that I'd be protected from selling my Soul. I definitely didn't know that my music would take as long as it did to finally find the ears of many listeners.

I was raised during the independent Golden era of music in the Bay Area. Independent music production was the way a young artist could essentially take a musical idea from nothing to something overnight, as long as he or she was willing to grind on the street about their music. As I was figuring out how to use my music equipment, I was still recording at other people's

31

studios to keep my chops wet. I began making mixtapes to sell on the street, not so much to create a buzz, but to actually make some income revenue. I figured the buzz would take care of itself.

Eventually, I joined forces with some patnas from high school and we began recording together. We formed a group called "The Unusual Suspects" under an imprint called "The Track Addictz" and pressed up our projects, selling copies of them all over the Bay Area, and anywhere we travelled to. I was still a solo artist at heart, but it felt cool to be working with my brothers who had the same pursuits that I had. We just wanted to make it together, so we all looked out for one another, and it seemed to be people around us who didn't like that.

There were certain elements to the music industry and the pursuits associated with it that could definitely bring out an unfavorable aspect of an individual's personality.

Fueled by memories of my early home life, and feeling alone in regards to achieving my dreams, I had to recognize a number of difficult truths. The first difficult truth was that my dreams were mine, and nobody else's. The idea I held in my mind that someone else would be willing to assist me along to reaching my goals would have to be erased. Everyone has dreams. At that time, I just thought that people assisted one another when the goals were clear and could benefit many. My dreams included financially taking care of my loved ones, and friends, as well as taking care of myself.

When I wasn't receiving the help I thought I should be receiving, there were moments where I kind of lost my way. I was engaging in low-vibratory, Spiritually debilitating actions that weren't serving the greater good. I was always covered from on High by my Angels and Ancestral Guides, but there were actions taken by myself, where if I wasn't extremely careful, even they would have to back away from protecting me. I wasn't recognizing the signs all around me that I should be taking my pursuits into another direction.

That I should be implementing a more positive energy into my sound.

By the time 2007 came along, I was fully accepting the life that I had experienced up to that moment. My home life was a literal mess, I was taken away from my home at fifteen years old because of it, I didn't have a consistent place to stay that I felt comfortable with, and whatever I was going to earn in life, I was going to earn it "on my own." I was lost. My life's path felt like it needing correcting, but I wasn't even in a state of mind to properly identify that need, let alone articulate that I needed it.

It was August 11, 2007 when the change my subconscious was yearning for arrived. I was at a showcase performing in Concord CA. It was a beautifully warm evening, and the sky was clear, revealing all of the glistening stars, even as the city lights shone brightly. I had just stepped off stage and decided to migrate to the grotto area of the establishment in order to get some fresh air and smoke a cigarette. I noticed a few people doing the same as I, so I made my way farther into the grotto by a tall, back wall that separated the street from the establishment.

As I sat down, back against the wall, I began to look up at the stars. I took a drag of my cigarette, slowly exhaling, and that is when I heard a voice. It wasn't in my ear like the voice I would hear some years later, but it was a voice that tapped into my mind; it was not my thought. It said "Jooge, if you keep doing what it is you're doing you're going to die." Just like that. Blunt as ever. I then saw the image of a road. It split out in front of me to form a fork with a large ivy plant separating the two directions. There were two directions for me to choose from. I could go "left" or I could go "right". Being left-handed I would normally have chosen the left-hand path, but something drew me to choose the right-hand path. The experience shook me to my core.

After the showcase on the way home, I told one of my group brothers what had happened. I told him that I wouldn't be pursuing music anymore. He almost stopped the car. I told him yeah Bruh, I just received a Spiritual message and I have to listen to it. He was silent. I made it home and walked inside my dads house. I pulled out my cushion pillows and situated them onto the floor with my blankets. I laid down. I had an extremely vivid dream of being in a home. The kitchen featured an open design, with an island in the middle. The kitchen door leading outside was kicked opened by police dressed in S.W.A.T. gear, looking like those from the film *The Matrix*. As they busted into the kitchen, I grabbed an MP5 submachine gun and started letting loose on them. They began firing back, hitting me several times. I could feel the sting and the heat from the bullets as they penetrated my astral body. I immediately woke up, taking a deep breath of air, attempting to sit up. As I breathed in I could still feel the heat from the bullets in my physical body. That's when I heard it for the third time in my life, the Devil's laugh, the same one on at the end of the hit-song "Thriller", except this time, it hadn't come through any sound-system or speakers; it was right outside my window. I rolled over out of the cushions as fast as I could and carefully pried open the bottom of the blinds. I saw nothing in the area where I felt that sound was coming from. I began to realize that my whole life, I'd been targeted, not because I was gifted and talented, and that people might be envious of that. Instead I finally realized that I was targeted because I was an important component to the ongoing Spiritual War raging all around us. I was being awakened to the Truth. The War is real and has always been. I'd just been so blinded by my early life experiences and associating them with my desire to leverage them into a Rap music career, that I didn't realize the truth of what was really going on. I wasn't being called to be another "Rapper". I was being called to be The Most High Mama & Papa's Ambassador here on earth!

When daylight arrived. I was led to prayer. Serious prayer. I was broken. I was contrite. I finally admitted my wrongful ways. I began to take accountability for them all. I finally knew how to think about my actions up to that point. I had caused pain to people, just as pain was caused to me. I focused on the pain I caused, taking accountability for it, and I forgave those who caused me pain; even if they never apologized. I began to lighten my load, releasing the burdens over my life. I went to my book bag, where I had kept all of my written lyrics and discs of music, released and unreleased. I looked through my notepads and all I could see that I had written was utter and complete trash. What I had written was perfect for the era and genres I had written the lyrics for, but they were distasteful and disrespectful to the Higher calling and purpose over my life. I gathered all of the papers and notepads, Cd's and promo materials, and went outside to the garbage bin, and threw everything away. I looked inside the the once empty bin, making sure everything landed into it, and closed the lid. As more trash and garbage began to pile on top of all of those lyrics and audio Cd's, I knew that was it, that was the end of a chapter of my life that sought to see me destroyed. I wasn't going to be turning back.

I had carried traumatic memories with me that fueled me to engage in low-vibrational activities in the pursuit of something I believed would make me feel better. I thought that once I reached my goals that I could simply repent for all of the wrong I'd committed in order to get to them, and that everything would be "okay". I didn't realize that "there" may not ever be reached, and therefore I may never repent. I'd just continue a disastrous cycle that I'd eventual fall victim to. Another one biting the dust.

I was blessed with the grace and mercy to wake up and see the error of my ways.

This was the beginning of the clutter, squalor, and hoarding within *my* mind, being identified and removed for good.

This was the beginning of the renewal of my mind.

3

"I'm Happy!"

Back in 1992 I was seven years old, and cast in a play called Cinderella. The character I was cast as was Happy, the fun-loving, glasses wearing dwarf of the Snow White and the Seven Dwarfs pantheon. Yes, you read that correctly; Happy somehow found his way into the universe of Cinderella and her precious glass slippers.

This play was different and presented a brand new comedic concept which we hadn't seen by combining the most popular Nursery Rhymes (and a couple not so popular ones), and having them all perform together on one stage, in one make-believe world. It would be almost a decade later when the idea was reintroduced on the Big Screen as the hit-movie *Shrek*.

Originally, I had hoped to be cast as the rapping Big Bad Wolf, and when I was cast as Happy, I was a little bummed out. The rapping Big Bad Wolf had really cool lines and, of course got to rap!

The lines, or shall I say line, written in the script for Happy was embarrassingly simple, but was to serve as a definite comedic break throughout the entire show.

I only had one job, but it was crucial to the upbeat energy of the show.

What was this infamous line that had everyone busting out with laughter each and every time I uttered it?

The line was simple: **"I'm happy"**

Yep, that was it. Not a word more or less. Just, "I'm happy".

Now you might be thinking to yourself "well what's so funny about that?".

First of all, let me be the first to admit that I thought the line was trash.

I came to that conclusion as an upset seven year old, angry because I didn't get the role I wanted and my mom was going to still make me participate in the play.

However, to my surprise, what that entire experience showed me was the importance of charisma and placement.

That simple two word line taught me that it's not what I say but how I say it, and that there is humor, warmth, and understanding in simplicity.

That line taught me to be grateful for what's bestowed upon me because it wasn't until I stepped on stage opening night, speaking my line for the very first time in front of a live audience, that I realized I *was* the correct choice for that role.

The moment I spoke that line "I'm happy", and received the loudest laughter I'd ever gotten in my entire life…it dawned upon me that I was originally upset at the role because I didn't understand the comedic psychological nuisances of that line and how the adults in the audience would perceive it.

If I had given in to my initial thoughts of quitting, I would've never experienced the joy of seeing a situation I doubted turn out to be so fun.

It turned out that the role was fun, and the play was a huge success.

When we look at the glass half full, we are able to begin recognizing a pattern of protection over our lives.

Things didn't seem to go our way until we stepped back from the situation, allowed it to play out, and came to the realization that the final result was actually something we'd be pleased with.

If we take an honest account of our personal journeys up to this point, we'd all agree that there are no coincidences in life, and that the unfoldment of your destiny has you exactly where you are supposed to be.

Let me tell you something: I've been blessed to learn through experience that it is such a joy to watch your child waking up with a smile on his or her face as the Sun rises to brighten the new day. It is also a joy to watch your child waking up with a smile on his or her face as the Sun rises to brighten the new day behind a bunch of rain-filled clouds.

To be truly happy, is to embrace a grateful mindset.

I had just lost my dear Uncle Eddie during this time of my life. He was a huge supporter and life-long fan of my young, little self. Uncle Eddie was one of my maternal great-uncles. This means that he was my maternal grandmothers uncle. He was actually my maternal great-grandmother Ella's, who was my maternal grandmother Emily's mom, little brother. To make it a little easier to grasp, Uncle Eddie was my moms moms moms little brother! He was fortunate to still be alive when I was born in 1985, and I was fortunate enough to have him in my life up until the time I was almost seven years old in 1992. As a matter of fact, I just celebrated his birthday on June 3, 2022 where he would've been 119 years old! Born in 1903, the youngest of six children, four girls and two boys, he was the "big little brother" who'd stepped up into a paternal role once their parents, and his older brother George Jr., passed away. His older sisters, one of which was my maternal great-grandmother Ella, were very fond of him, and saw him as their hero. He was tall too, about 6'5", with a smooth caramel-complexion, and high cheekbones, surely inherited from our indigenous ancestors and ancestress's of the Washitaw Nation located in northern Louisiana. I have been blessed to have inherited many of the same features and characteristics as him. My middle name is also his namesake. Uncle Eddie truly was a great man.

A shoe cobbler by trade, Uncle Eddie was a hard working, diligent man, who owned his home located in South Richmond CA. He wore suspenders and his pants were from a time almost forgotten by most today. Children today would only get to see the types of threads he wore in a museum or in some stash of old clothes located in an attic filled with family heirlooms of a bygone era. Before he passed, my mother, thinking ahead, asked him for a series of his older clothing, which included some blazer jackets, suit pants and a pair or two of his suspenders; he loved his suspenders. He happily obliged. I had no idea she was asking for these items so that I could one day put them on as part of my costume for the first live- play I'd soon be acting in. She obviously had to tailor them for my short body, seeing that Uncle Eddie was so tall, and I was nowhere near his height at that time. She outfitted me with his suit jacket, dress shirt, suit pants and suspenders. To top off this hilariously looking ensemble, she went to the local thrift-store and found some large-sized, leather dress shoes, that I could wear. I looked like a little man. I had to be careful when I walked because if I took a misstep and began to stumble, someone might mistake me for a Little Person who'd have had a bit too much alcohol to drink at the local bar, also known as a pub by many.

I made people smile with curiosity everywhere I'd go during the days of my rehearsals. Even though I was originally skeptical about participating in the play, and would rather play outside with my friends in the neighborhood, I began to truly appreciate the experience. There were however, a couple of defining moments that would take place during the preparation for this play that would shape and mold me into the teenager I'd become, as well as into the man I am today.

To fully grasp the insight provided within the pages of this book, you have to remember that everything happens for a reason. It is not my aim to victimize myself and seek your pity.

I was new to show-business. I had never auditioned for a role before. I didn't know how to present myself, or what to expect from the casting director, who was also the writer and director of the play. I had also never seen so many girls in one place at one time. Everywhere I seemed to look, there was a pretty little girl, my age, that I could daydream about. I was already talking to the girls in my grade at school, and sometimes in the grade above, trying to get one of them to be my girlfriend! I was a little Casanova in the making for sure hahaha. I've always loved the protective responsibility a young man, or man, was supposed to exhibit when taking care of his girlfriend, wife, or wives. These traits were engraved into my DNA, no more than a young Lion cub feels the need to welp, practicing its roar, which will one day mightily, reverberate throughout the land for all to be subject to.

The day of auditions finally arrived and the only thing that helped me combat the desire to stay at home and play outside with the neighborhood children, was that one of my dear friends at the time, Desanté, who I'd known since kindergarten, would be auditioning too. My dad was never involved with any of my extra-curricular activities unless they were sports related. Even then, his actual involvement was limited to driving me to practice, or attending one of my baseball games. Once I could walk the streets by myself however, him driving me to practice and games pretty much ended. He would also play catch with us. I was grateful for what he did do, but I knew there was another level to a dad's involvement in his child's life that I wasn't receiving. I accepted what he gave me though because at least it was something. Many

40

of the children in my Hood didn't have their fathers with them at all, so I was different in that respect. I happily shared my dad with many of my friends. My mother loaded me into her car, and we headed to Hogan High School, where the auditions would be held. They were actually conducted in the school cafeteria, which we realized upon arrival. When we arrived to the audition, my mother revealed to me that she would be dropping me off, then leaving to handle an errand in the area, and that she'd be back before auditions were over; I should've known at that moment that by myself I'd be the one to have to experience this "thing" through. I thought she'd at least stay while I experienced my first audition. She signed my name onto the clipboard, and briefly spoke with the director. While she was chatting with the director, I was able to locate my buddy Desanté and we began kicking it, waiting for the audition to officially begin. After her and the director's conversation, she came over to me, informing me that she'd be back before the audition was over. I don't recall her giving me any advice, besides the generic "do your best". We surely hadn't practiced or rehearsed at home for what could potentially transpire during the audition. I did my best as I was instructed. My friend Desanté being at auditions with me, really kept me calm and collected. I learned how important it could be to identify a "familiar face" that day.

There were many roles to fill. One of which was the Rapping Big Bad Wolf. That role caught my eye immediately and I wanted it. Desanté agreed that I would be great for the role because he was a witness to my rapping skills while we'd be playing on the playground at school. Wanting that role so badly took my mind off of my mother leaving to handle errands. I felt like I could facilitate that role flawlessly because of my ever-increasing Rap skills. I had no idea about stage-presence and articulation though. I also wasn't too tall or big physically. The role ended up going to an older child named Josh. Josh's mother stayed at the audition with him too. Even though I desperately wanted that role, he would go on to do very well and prove he was the right person for the job. I was eventually cast as Happy, one of the more joyous members of the Seven Dwarfs pantheon.

After auditions, I said "see ya bro" to Desanté, as his mother walked through the door to pick him up. The next week at school he'd inform me that he would be moving from Vallejo, and transferring schools. I was sad about my friend leaving. We'd been tight since kindergarten, at a Christian private school named Noah's Ark. This also meant that he wasn't going to be participating in the play any longer, so now, I had no friends who'd be acting in the play with me. Desanté left our elementary school at the end of the school year, and the next time I'd see him, was at a McDonald's after my Uncle Eddie's funeral and burial in Richmond CA about a month later. As close as Uncle Eddie and I were, my mother did not allow me to go inside the funeral. I was heartbroken. I had to wait outside in my dads van with his friend E.T. while the funeral took place. My cousins were able to go inside the church for the funeral processions, and we were very close in age, my cousins and I, so I was confused as to why I couldn't attend as well. This was my dear Uncle Eddie after all. What made this particular day more interesting is that I brutally told E.T. that I wished he'd died instead. I am still sorry for making that statement to him. After the funeral, we went to the burial site at Rolling Hills Cemetery. The family was hungry and decided on eating at the McDonald's located across the road from the cemetery. My dad couldn't stand McDonald's, his reason being that "they put worms in the burgers". Well, if it wasn't for him getting outvoted, we'd have never went to that McDonald's and I wouldn't have seen, of all people, my good friend Desanté, who I hadn't seen or spoken to since the last day of school, standing in line asking for a drink refill! We were so thrilled to see one another, it was Divine Timing at its finest. I sure was happy to be at Mickey D's that day, because it would be the official last time I'd see my friend. We couldn't have seen each other at a more perfect time.

Once I knew what to begin expecting from the play production, I began to put my best foot forward, reading the script and familiarizing myself with the story-line. As a child I was extremely interested in the supernatural, as well as paranormal phenomena. When I'd visit a library, I'd always be led to the supernatural and occult section of books. I didn't even know what "occult" meant during those days, but those books truly peaked my interest. Where other children might be afraid of what they'd find within the pages of those books, I was curious at what I'd find and read, learning about everything from Bigfoot, fairies, and witches, to vampires, ghosts and the Loch Ness Monster. I even began reading the original Snow White and The Seven Dwarfs story, as recorded by the Brothers Grimm, so that I could be acclimated to the "real" narrative. I began to realize how different the play I was participating in was from the original story, as well as from the version released by Disney.

Once production of the play officially began, we would have many rehearsals. I remember the director being very "no-nonsense", demanding us to be absolute professionals. I think that it may be a bygone ear in this new millennium, but in the early nineties, people still held a strong belief in "there's no business like show business". Each day, I would go to school, and then come home to do whatever homework I'd be able to crank out. Whenever it was time go, my mom would walk me to the car, and open the door to let me get inside of it, making sure she didn't shut the door onto my fingers. Then she'd open her door, and sit down inside, making sure we were both buckled up safely; then we'd pull off to get me to rehearsal. Once we'd get to the school parking lot, she'd swiftly pull up as closely as she could to the entrance door. I'd get out and say bye to her, then she'd pull off to go run an errand. Full dress rehearsals would prove to be very interesting. The day finally came when it was time to wear Uncle Eddie's old clothing. I was excited to put that costume on, I won't even lie. I dressed up, pulling those old britches up, strapping my suspenders on, and buttoning my dress shirt. Then I'd place those large shoes onto my feet, grab my copy of the script and get into character.

The day of my first rehearsal was a disaster. I was super excited, and my mom had somewhere else to be. When she dropped me off, I joyously ran into the hallway leading to the school auditorium. However, something felt "off", as soon as I walked through those doors. There were a bunch of people walking throughout the halls that I'd never seen before. I thought they were the unseen parents of the older children who were "too mature" for their mothers to show up to rehearsals. I didn't notice a single face, and to make matters worse, I couldn't locate any of my peers who'd normally be in the places I checked before rehearsals began. By the time I realized there was another event being held that evening instead of dress rehearsal, my mother had pulled off!

I grew frantic. Here I was, this little boy, dressed in a costume that, from a distance, made me look like a Little Person who'd just had a rough night at the bar and had lost his way home, somehow stumbling into an evening-time event taking place in a high school auditorium to possibly start some trouble. When the adults walking down the hallway realized I was actually a little boy, they presumed that I was purposely dressed the way I was because those were the only clothes I had to wear; they knew absolutely nothing about dress rehearsal that evening. No one knew how I'd gotten to the school either. Many people gawked at me, smiling hilariously, and pointing in my direction saying things like "Oh wow, look at that little man!" and "Mommy, why is he dressed like that?" As I made my way down the hallway, still checking to see if maybe the rehearsal had gotten relocated to make room for the event taking place in the auditorium, I realized there was a pay phone that I might be able to use to call my parents. I knew how to use the phone book from all of my days spent playing on Uncle Eddie's living room floor. He always kept a phone book. I learned my ABC's from memorizing the little tabs along the sides of the pages of the old school phone books from the 1980's. My parents had always listed our Alameda number in the phone book back then, so I figured I'd try my luck and see if they were listed inside of the Vallejo version. When I was done making my final rounds, and confirmed that the dress rehearsal was really canceled, I made my way back to the pay phone.

The phone book was weighty, and was attached to one of those heavy-duty binders that kept the book from being taken from the pay phone system. I opened it up and looked for our last name. Once I located my parents and identified our phone number, I realized I didn't have any coinage! How was I going to place this call?! That's when I totally lost it and began to cry. I didn't know how to place a "collect call" in those days. I began walking up and down the hallway looking for anyone who might have some spare change, but no one could help me. As I was crying, a kind young lady walking up the hallway, probably sixteen or seventeen years old, noticed me crying and obviously frazzled. She stopped and asked me if she could help me. I said "yes please" as I fought back the tears, sniffing profusely as little children who've become upset do. She asked me if I knew my phone number and I told her yes. She reached into her pocket and retrieved a quarter so that we could make the phone call. Once she placed that quarter into the phone, and began dialing my number, I felt a wave of relief come over me; I was about to be picked up and taken home! As the phone rang, we waited for someone to answer it on the other end. No one answered. I knew the possibility of no one answering the phone because my dad would always allow the answering-machine to catch the call, and then he'd pick up the phone if it was someone he actually wanted to talk to. It was his version of caller-ID before caller-ID was actually released to the general public for use. When no one answered the phone, I was forced to leave a message. I had hoped that once they heard my sad sounding voice, someone would pick up the phone, and comfort me, saying "ok son, we're on the way!", but still, no answer. The young lady was patient, bless her heart. I told her that my parents don't usually pick up the phone so we would have to leave another message. She reached into her pocket, grabbing her last quarter, and we tried the call again. This time she waited as the phone rang. Once the answering-machine kicked in, she left the message. I always had a thing for the older girls, and her ability to compassionately and professionally handle the situation provided me some comfort that everything would be okay.

My dad would usually be outside in the front of the house hanging with his buddy's talking about work, or any other thing that entered into their adult minds. He must've heard the call this time, as he came inside to use the bathroom to relieve himself, because he picked up the phone as the young lady was leaving her message. Once she confirmed that he was my dad, she handed me the phone, and waited while I spoke to him. I told him that dress rehearsal was canceled and that I needed to be picked up because no one from the production was at the school. He told me that my mom was still out running her errands, and that he didn't know how to get to the school so I'd have to wait for her to get home, and then he'd send her to come and get me; go figure! Drying my eyes, still sniffling, I told him "okay, I'll wait for her", but in my mind I was like, "you gotta be kidding me." I told the young lady who had assisted me that my mom would be on the way, but I don't know when. She then informed that she had to go back to the auditorium to conclude her evening at the event she was actually at the school for. Before she walked away she led me to the concession snack table, and kindly asked the lady collecting money if she'd be willing to give me a candy bar while I waited for my mom. The candy lady could clearly see I was upset about something, so she allowed me to pick a candy bar; I chose a Snickers. I told the candy lady thank you. As the young girl led me back towards the hallway entrance door so I could see my mom pulling up, I told her thank you as well. She gave me instructions on where I should stand. "Don't go outside, just stand right here in the doorway, and wait until you see your mom, then go outside." I told her "okay", then she walked back into the auditorium. As I waited for my mom, enjoying the Snickers I had been given, the event began to wrap up.

The parking lot lights and the street lights began to turn on. It must've taken my mom the better part of thirty minutes to finally arrive. If I was supposed to be at dress rehearsal for an hour and a half, she returned about five minutes after the originally scheduled rehearsal time. Once she pulled into the parking lot I just shook my head in disapproval. She told me she was sorry, and I wanted to believe her. She also told me that she was still running errands and had only gone home to drop off whatever items she had purchased to make room in the car for me when it was time to pick me up. Had she not gone home, she wouldn't have known I needed her to pick me up early. I guess it really didn't matter because she arrived when she could. Honestly, I wanted to go home, take my Uncle Eddie's clothes off, and never go back to that school again. My mom told me that if I run the remainder of her errands with her, that she'd allow me to pick out a small toy, so I stayed in the car and journeyed to her next destination with her. When we arrived at Thrifty's with me, still dressed like a little man, I immediately went to the toy aisle, and I chose a hand-held video game made by Tiger Co.. It was a Magic Johnson vs Larry Bird "Basketball Shootout" game. I made sure that it had batteries and that it turned on, then I located my mom, told her "thank you", and completed shopping with her.

When we finally got home, and pulled up, I noticed my dad sitting in one of his military school buses he had purchase a month or two prior. The military complex on Mare Island was liquidating many of its military vehicles in preparation for an eventual shutdown of the base. My dad caught wind of this and went bonkers, purchasing as many Jeep's, buses, and semi trucks as he could. In essence, he wasn't technically busy, he just couldn't pick me up because he "didn't know" where the school was located. I went inside and took off my costume. I hung the ensemble up on the hangers that Uncle Eddie had given to us, and I went to open the packaging of my new toy. Once the packaging was opened, I went outside to play with it, sitting in my dads school bus as I learned the games button functions.

The remainder of the dress rehearsals would go on without hitch, and everyone in the production grew in confidence that we'd be able to pull this play off. Finally, the first day of the play had arrived, and it was showtime. I was excited and a little anxious. I'm pretty sure I had the shortest lines in the whole script, but they were to pack the biggest punch. Seeing as it was my first play, I wasn't aware that I could actually get dressed into my costume backstage. I got dressed into my costume at home and just showed up ready to go and perform. Witnessing each performer getting ready backstage was an experience in and of itself. It was like being in a house while everyone was getting ready to go trick-or-treating on Halloween. I had arrived in full costume regalia, ready to step on stage.

Some of the girls, unbeknownst to me, were still in their nighties, so when I walked backstage, I immediately stepped my little self back out until it was cool for me to come back in. Upon my reentry into the backstage area, I noticed all of the parents getting their children ready, and I thought to myself why isn't my mom back here with me? Yes, my mom had dropped me off again! She told me she had to go back home to finish getting ready, and that she wanted to borrow my Uncle Ronald's camcorder so that she could film the play. I thought to myself, "okay, I guess being filmed is a cool trade for her leaving me here again, so alright, go ahead." This next series of events would prove to be defining moments in my life. As I sauntered thru the backstage area, looking for the other dwarfs, I was pulled to the side by one of the older children and her mom. They noticed that I was in full costume already, but informed me that "I was missing something". They told me that I needed to put on makeup so that I could get "all the way into character." It must be noted that I was the only little Indigenous ("Black") boy in the entire play. I also wasn't aware of the emasculation of Indigenous males at that time. I vehemently refused. I might not of been the better part of seven years old, but I knew that I was not going to be putting any makeup on my face, nor was I going to allow makeup to be put onto my face.

I have always been blessed with Divine Wisdom. The feeling that came over me when I was propositioned to place makeup on my face was a very uncomfortable one. When I refused the first time, I thought that would be it. As I walked away from them, and over to my group of fellow dwarfs, I was propositioned again. This time with even more persuasive tactics. Now it was my fellow dwarfs, all girls, who really tried to make me feel as though I was an inadequate actor for not wanting to put makeup onto my eyes and lips! When I refused again, all I could think about was "I'm not gay" and why all of a sudden no one wanted to be my friend, as if my not putting makeup on my face was going to affect the outcome of the production negatively. They began to point out Josh, the actor who won the role of Big Bad. They showed me how he had on makeup and was cool with it, and that he was a boy, so I should be cool with it too. As I looked Josh's face over, I immediately realized the half-truths they were illustrating to me. First off, Josh was supposed to look like a wolf. Out of all of the roles, he was supposed to look the least human-like. The "makeup" on his face was actually face paint, painted on by his mother, and made to look like a wolf, with a gray snout, whiskers, and furry patches that were strategically placed along his jawline and cheekbones. He looked like he was getting ready for a pretty fun Halloween party. What he didn't have on his face was the eye-shadow and lipstick that the girls and that one mother were attempting to put onto my face.

When I refused their advances for the third and final time, I became the Enemy of the State. We got the call from the director that it was time for the curtain to raise, and that the show would begin. The girls distanced themselves from me, and I was more grateful than anything. The pressure was finally off of me. I did wish my mom was backstage with me, and I always felt that they wouldn't have tried that if she had been. I wasn't able to inform my mom of what happened until after the play. It's even more wild because she arrived back to play well into the first act, and when she finally sat down to begin filming the play, she forgot to take the lens cap off of the camcorder. She didn't realize this until the last 20-25 minutes of the play though. At least the camcorder microphone worked, so the audio was captured, and you could still hear the audience cracking up with laughter every time I spoke those infamous lines: "I'm Happy!"

The production lasted for five days. Mom was able to borrow the camcorder one more time, and she finally captured the footage of the play. The show was a success and I never allowed anyone to put makeup on my face. I was a true little man. I had maintained my dignity and my respect. By the end of it all, the girls, my fellow dwarfs, weren't upset with me, and we were able to stand hand-in-hand and take our bows. We received a standing ovation from all spectators. The overall experience added to my level of confidence moving forward through life.

Now, I've matured some, having been blessed with a fully locked beard, and the great stature of a Divine God Man in this realm, and I still, after all of this time, have not put makeup onto my face.

49

4

"Who Ya Gonna Call? Listen, and Hear Me..."

"**N**o harm will overtake you,
     no disaster will come near your tent.
     For He will command His angels concerning you
to guard you in all your ways;
they will lift you up in their hands,
  so that you will not strike your foot against a stone." - *Psalm 91:10-12*

My Angels...

  Chuck E. Cheese
   Neighborhood Angel
   Bedroom Angel
   Alley Angel
   "Willie Jean Thompson"

My entire life has been comprised of supernatural and paranormal events that I always accepted as being real and true. I never was one of those types to doubt the spiritual realm and its many nuanced layers. I suppose, believing in a realm outside of this one, helped me get through my most darkest days in some way. By the time I touched down to the earth realm, the film *Ghostbusters* had a good year's worth of a solid run before I was made privy to its existence. The hit theme-song written and performed by Ray Parker, Jr. is still a monumental classic, inspiring modern Ghostbusters all over the world, and giving new life to the meaning "I ain't 'fraid of no ghost". If Twitter existed while growing up through the late eighties, and especially the nineties, the question "have you ever seen a ghost?" would've been a trending topic for sure. Back in those days the world was witnessing a shift. The technology boom of the eighties had begun to take hold of the global society, with many people finally being in financial position to afford the many gidgets and gadgets tech companies had to offer. We were all experiencing a major shift in how the world was operating daily. There were however, still many pockets of people throughout the land, that hadn't experience the tech boom yet, and who weren't missing out either. It's funny and ironic to think about, but there was a time when those who had technology were the weirdo oddballs. Now it's the other way around; those who don't have technology are considered the weirdo oddballs.

One evening, while my parents were away on a double-date with my Uncle Keith and Auntie Ro to dinner at the "Gingerbread House", an upscale Cajun restaurant located in an old Victorian-styled home in Oakland, I saw my first apparition. I was two years old. This would be the first apparition I can fully remember. I was being babysat by my neighbor's daughter. She was a musically inclined, sixteen year old young lady named Nikki. She would sometimes be hired by my mom to watch me whenever my parents took a night on the town. Once my brother was born in 1987, Nikki would occasionally be hired to look after us both. The event I'm about to describe took place in my life before we moved to Vallejo, and before the birth of my sister in 1991. I want to say it happened in the early part of 1988.

Nikki was a flutist. She also owned a new, full-scale Casio keyboard that came packed with many sound kits and a digital screen. Back in the eighties, if you owned one of these types of keyboards, you were to be respected, and

51

were seen as one who took their musical craft seriously. I looked up to Nikki. She is the one who gave me my life-long nickname Jujee.

On this evening, my mom and dad were very excited to go to dinner. They loved eating at the Gingerbread House. Every time they'd go to dine there, my mom would bring me back a large, freshly baked gingerbread cookie with a hard heart candy infused into the bellybutton region of the cookie. Icing would would be used to decorate the other elements of the cookie person, making the final outcome a culinary work of art. Whenever they ate dinner at the "Gingerbread House" I knew the chances of me getting a sweet treat would be high, so I wouldn't mind being left behind while they had their fun for the evening. It was a decent trade-off to me. I always wanted to eat there though, but never got the opportunity to do so. T.J.'s Gingerbread House was a Cajun restaurant, tea house, and gift shop that operated for 36 years, closing in 2007. I'm not sure why I didn't visit on my own, once I got old enough to. The location was a Bay Area staple, and was a very popular place to dine.

When my parents left, they informed Nikki that we had already eaten, but that if we wanted a snack, we could have some of the Wheat-Thins that were in the cabinet until they returned. We said our "see ya laters" and my parents left, gently shutting the front door behind themselves. Once they were gone, I immediately asked Nikki if I could play her keyboard. She would bring it over knowing that I'd want to play it. She obliged and I sat down on the floor, plugged it into the wall socket, and powered it on. She asked me to turn down the volume though. Soul Train was a super popular show in those days, and it just so happened to be on t.v., so when Nikki turned it on, she naturally wanted to watch it with as little added distraction as possible.

I began to play the keyboard, but I wasn't to thrilled that I had to keep the volume low. I'd usually be allowed to crank it up and play to my hearts content. As Nikki watched her show, I grew bored at playing the keyboard in such a low decibel, so I turned it off, and went to sit on the couch by her. My little brother turned one year old in February. This is significant because my mom didn't feel comfortable leaving us both to go on a date until he was a little older. While he was a newborn my mom would take him with her if she had to leave me with Nikki for any extended period of time. I'm pretty sure this was my moms first real date since he'd been born. That's why her and my dad were so excited.

Once the credits started to roll, and the show went off, I asked Nikki if I could watch cartoons. I had no idea that it was a doubleheader! I liked Soul Train and all, but a back-to-back show? I was a toddler, it was natural for me to want to watch cartoons. However, what I loved about Soul Train at that young stage of my life was the opening sequence. It featured a colorfully animated cartoon train that flowed with the sounds of Soul and Funk music, taking a ride through the production set, and then rolling away until it "faded into the distance." Young people would be grooving and moving to the intro music, and Don Cornelius, the shows long-standing host, would greet everyone, including the viewers, with his trademarked baritone voice and cool, well-patted Afro. The show really was a great success.

My little brother had been taking an evening nap in our bedroom. I decided that I should get up to go check on him. We'd normally keep the hallway light on, and our bedroom door open, so that light from the hallway would emanate into our room. We stayed in an upstairs unit of the Buena Vista Apartments off of Webster street, and it could get quite hot some days, so keeping the majority of our lights turned off was a wise strategy to keep the heat down. When I entered into the bedroom, I realized that my brother was still napping, and that I wanted to lay down next to him and relax as well until our parents returned from dinner. I climbed carefully into bed, with my back resting against my pillow and the wall. I would normally sleep near the edge of the bed, by the door. That evening wasn't any different. I glanced towards my left to take one more look at my baby brother, before attempting to nod off myself. As I lay down beginning to relax, eyelids open and still hearing the second episode of Soul Train broadcasting in the living room, I saw something appear at the foot of my bed. I've always been an inquisitive person, but I decided to hold my position in bed, and analyze whatever this was, from where I was. As I carefully watched this being begin to peek it's head up from the foot of the bed, I noticed how much it looked and seemed to move, like a famous comic book character I was familiar with: Spider-Man. This entity was very different than any Spider-Man I had seen though. For starters, it didn't speak; all it appeared to do was look towards my direction, and tilt the top part of its head left to right in a slow but steady motion. Spider-Man has always had something witty to say. The second odd thing about the entity was that it was completely black. Not "clothing black", but "shadow black". The two things it had in common with Spider-Man was its apparent body shape, and the way it moved. Imagine someone on their knees while on the floor, at the foot of your bed, then beginning to lift themselves up and closer to you, while gripping the blanket or sheet on your bed to pull themselves up onto the mattress. I waited no more than 10-12 seconds before jetting up out my room, leaving my brother behind. As I ran into the living room area, and saw Nikki, sitting nonchalantly on the couch; I immediately informed her as to what I'd just seen. She told me to back to the room and get my brother. By the time I made it back into the bedroom, the Shadow Entity, as I called it to this day, had disappeared and my brother was sitting up, awake, in bed. I asked him if he saw the "ghost", to which he replied "no". I told him "come on" and he left with me out of the bedroom and into the living room. When our parents walked through the front door after having returned from their date, I immediately ran up to them and told them about what I had seen. I noticed a bewildering look on my mom's face. She was carrying the world-famous Gingerbread House baggie that carried within it a gingerbread man. She told me to allow her and my dad to come inside, pay Nikki for her services, and then get settled in before she'd give us our cookie. Once settled in, and Nikki had left home, I told her about what I had seen. I think my mom thought I was too young for her to explain to me what it was I had seen, or at the very least, too young for her to explain supernatural concepts that were outside of the movies and in real time. She handed me my cookie in hopes that I'd switch subjects. I took my cookie, and while I was taking my first bite of it, I asked her if we, meaning my brother and I, could sleep in her and my dad's bedroom. We ended up having to sleep in our room that night, but it was one of the first nights I remember saying the "Now I lay me down to sleep" prayer.

I didn't have any bad dreams during sleep that night. I would however, go on to have many supernatural experiences throughout my life though. I've always been connected to that frequency and dimension beyond the veil of our physical realm. I've always felt "the other side" knowing that just beyond our own perception and awareness, there are realms that can be acknowledged and tapped into. Often, these realms seem to have greater access to ours, or maybe, we've been numbed to their existence by the film industry and the media, making us believe that these realms do not truly exist and are mere figments of our imaginations.

When I was about four months old, my dads mom passed away. She was living in Chicago when he got the news. My dad has never liked flying on airplanes, so he booked some train tickets and we took an Amtrak to The Windy City. It was November, so you can imagine that it was just beginning to get chilly. I don't remember the train ride much, but I do remember my grandmothers funeral. We sat towards the front of the church while the celebration of life was taking place. My Uncle John, her eldest son, and my dads big brother, was the officiating Minister. Uncle John has always been the "family pastor", and has done a great job leading and guiding many people to the Truth of the Most High. Even though he founded one of the largest churches in Chicago, he remains a very humble man. I was held tightly by mother during the funeral. She had me swaddled most of the ceremony, with my back on her lap, causing me to look up towards the church ceiling. As I looked up, I could see angels. Literal angels, flying around the ceiling of the church. They were a glow of yellowish-white light, and they would fly, stop for a moment, appear to be looking down towards all of us in the church, and then begin flying again. I wasn't speaking audible English yet, but I'm sure I would have told my parents to "look up" if I could. I think that was also kind of the point of the angels revealing themselves to me; I was only supposed to "watch them", and not "talk about them" at that moment in time. I've always remembered that experience though.

The following section of this book, will address a few, not all, but a few more of the major supernatural and angelic phenomena that occurred in my life. Two of the occurrences took place during my childhood, which harbored some of the darkest moments in my life. The other two occurrences took place as I was beginning to be ushered into a season of introspection, finally making sense of what I'd experienced throughout my life; not quite healed from the trauma, but on my way to healing.

Chuck E. Cheese

One day when I was in the fourth grade, my mom allowed all of us to stay home from school.

My siblings and I asked her if we could go someplace. We felt like we were "pushing our limits" in asking, but we mustered up the courage, and requested if we could go to Chuck E. Cheese, the children's fun center, where "A Kid Can Be A Kid". "Kids" are baby goats, so that slogan still kinda throws me off just thinking about it. As she considered our request, she began to layout some ground rules if she was to take us. She told us that we'd only have a certain allotment of tokens, and that once they were spent, we could stay a little longer to play in the "slide and ball pit", and then it'd be time to go. We were happy with that deal because we had never been to Chuck E. Cheese during school hours and we knew that once we made it inside the building, we'd be some of the only children, if not the only children, there at that time. We agreed to her stipulations. She picked up a phone book, which had been a copy of one of the recently released phone books that everyone in the community would receive yearly. Locating the phone number, she then called to make sure they were open. She sat down on a pile of papers she'd been "saving" and dialed the number while we anxiously sat in the living room wherever we could to await the confirmation that we'd be able to make the trip to Chuck E. Cheese. Someone at the restaurant gave us the "Ok" to come on by, so we cheered in excitement and began making our way outside to the vehicle we'd be using that day.

My mom asked my dad if she could drive his van. He agreed, and then we piled in and hit the road. When we arrived to Chuck E. Cheese's, we were indeed the only children there. Whenever we went somewhere with my mom, we knew we were to be on our best behavior. Mom went to the ticket center and asked for a cup of tokens, and led us to the seating area to distribute a cut to each of us.

I must state for the record, that it was outings and moments like these that really confused me. One minute my mom could be a really sweet "mom" and the next it was like I didn't even recognize her. When we were out in public, and so well behaved, it made my mom look good in the eyes of others. If we had acted like how she did when we were together at home, no one would want us to patron their establishments. In public, we wore a mask for her sake, but when we got home it was difficult, if not impossible, for her to wear a mask for ours. I didn't realize until later on in life that this behavior wasn't normal, and that she really did need some psychological help with clearing and re-harmonizing the spaces in her mind. I still pray for her daily.

We each took our little cut of tokens happily and commenced to playing the arcade games that we liked the most. I specifically remember looking at my stash of tokens, thinking how I better ration what I have so that I can play some of the games that dispense tickets. I really liked going to the ticket center before leaving to trade them in for a prize or two. When I got down to my last few tokens, I realized that I'd better go and play those ticket dispensing games, so that is what I did. I was able to collect a few tickets, but nothing substantial enough to trade them in for a large item. I folded them up and placed them into my pocket. I then located my younger siblings, and we went over to the slide and ball pit to play within that structure. Our time at Chuck E. Cheese for the day was soon to come to an end. We wrapped up playing in the ball pit, and made our way to the ticket center.

When we arrived at the ticket center, we immediately recognized how quite everything was. We were used to a long line of children waiting their turn to choose what special prizes they were going to go home with. That particular day, there wasn't any of that energy. Instead, there was one young man, an Asian man, whom had positioned himself to assist us. As we made our way up to him, glancing into the glass prize stations to begin picking our prizes, we realized that we simply didn't have enough tickets individually to pick the items that we really wanted. We began to contemplate if we should bunch our tickets together and share one large prize, which still, wouldn't have been that "large" because we didn't have enough for any of the items shelved on the wall behind him. That's where all of the "big" prizes were.

He overheard us going back and forth about what we should do, and motioned for us all to come up to him. Now, this guy wasn't old at all. I want to say he was about 24-28 years old. I mention his age because he didn't have to be as kind as he was, and he didn't have to resonate with what we were going through. He could've been impatient and rushed us to make our decision so that he could go back to doing whatever it was he was doing before we arrived to the ticket center. He looked like a normal guy. He came out of a door that was open from back behind the prize station. He was dressed in his purple Chuck E. Cheese team shirt. We were literally the only children in the whole establishment, and he seemed to be the only employee on duty that day. He asked each of us how many tickets we had, and we told him our ticket count. He then told us we could put all of our tickets together and get one large item to share, or we could keep our tickets separate, and each get a number of smaller items. We decided to keep our tickets separate, and each chose smaller items, which seemed to be the better deal because as we looked at the shelved items, they truly weren't as appealing as they'd normally be. We were super happy that we received a chance to choose many different smaller items, which costed way more than the amount of tickets we each had. This guy was cool! He was really hooking us up!

Once we were done choosing our prizes, grinning widely from ear to ear, we told the young man thank you many times, and even turned around waving to him as we walked out of the establishment happy that it was he who had helped us. We were never treated to such kindness at a Chuck E. Cheese before. We each walked out with a prize bag full of goodies that we would've normally never received with the amount of tickets we actually had. We felt so blessed.

As we piled into the van and my mom began driving us back to Vallejo, we knew we were going to have to call Chuck E. Cheese once we made it home. We felt an overwhelming desire to make our gratitude known to management. We hadn't seen a manager that earlier in the day but we figured that before the late afternoon-evening shift began, we'd be able to contact one. We wanted to let someone know how much we appreciated the service that day and how they should commend the young man who assisted us so kindly. We made it home safely and walked inside to begin playing with our new toys. My mom decided that she should call Chuck E. Cheese as soon as we got home, while it was fresh on her mind to do so. It was mid-afternoon, well before any evening shift would begin clocking in. She sat down on that same pile of papers she'd been "saving" and grabbed the phone book again. She located the number once more, and called Chuck E. Cheese.

As she was calling, we all slightly stopped what we were doing in order to ear-hustle her conversation. She began speaking with someone on the other end, stating how much we had a great time, and how the kind young man had truly made our day and experience special. The person on the phone with her, began to inquire about what exactly had happened because it was definitely against company protocol for a Chuck E. Cheese employee to be so "giving". I could tell my mom was slightly reluctant to describe the young man who had assisted us in fear he might get reprimanded, but she continued describing him. She finished describing him, when all of a sudden she formed a shocked look on her face. The person on the other end of the phone asked her to describe the young man one more time and if she could provide his name. That's when it dawned on us, that we never asked the young man his name. My mom told the person that we didn't know his name, but described him to a T. Note that it only took us about twenty minutes to get home, and she immediately made the phone call, so any shift-changes were highly unlikely. The evening time crew definitely would not have clocked in yet. After listening carefully to my mom's description of the young man, the person on other end of the phone, uneasily stated "no one by that description works here mam." My mom looked towards us, and then spoke into the phone headset asking the person to repeat themselves. Again, they said "no one by that description works here mam, and we've been the only ones here all morning." My mom asked "are you sure?". The person replied "yes". She kindly ended the conversation and hung the phone up. She then informed us that the young man wasn't even employed at Chuck E. Cheese, and that no one had ever seen a person matching the description we provided. She also told us that the person on the phone said that there were other employees at Chuck E. Cheese working that day, and that we just "hadn't seen them".

We all agreed that afternoon that who we encounter was an Angel. That we had been rewarded for being obedient to our mom, and for being on our best behavior.

Neighborhood Angel

I'm really from the Hood like that stringy piece.

Day by day, I'd find ways to adjust to life in the environment I was raised in. I can still hear my dad's voice loudly in my mind, telling my brother, cousin, and I: "If you ever smoke crack I'm gonna shoot you dead in Yo a**." As we made our way to the grocery store, we sat in the back seat of my dads car, looked at each other and started to giggle under our breath thinking "ummm excuse me sir, but you don't need to threaten us with violence or death…we see what crack is doing to our community, and we aint finna touch that mess!" He felt like he had to say those words to us though. It was a real trip because all the dromers and addicts were his friends. He was one of the few Black men in the Hood who wasn't strung out on dope, and he took great advantage of this. He would oftentimes hire folks in the Hood to do odd jobs and tasks that he either felt were beneath him, or that he didn't want to make time for. Many people were on dope. Because of this, many people always needed a fix. My dad would hire addicts for a couple dollars a job. I guess he figured that he wasn't "going to enable them fully", so he'd give them just enough to get a quick hit. If they were studious workers, maybe they'd get hired by another "sober" mind who'd be willing to exploit them for services as well. We always had dogs as I was coming up. Big dogs. My dad was into Rottweilers. Our first dog was a large black Labrador-Rottweiler mix named Rocky that he purchased from a flea market. He was all black but had a large Rottweiler frame. He was actually very friendly and a pretty cool dog. He was our first dog as a family. Just like any animal, dogs eat, and dogs relieve themselves. I always wanted to work for allowance but my dad wouldn't allow it. Instead he'd hire one of the addicts in the neighborhood to come by and pick up the dog poop for a dollar or two. I'm wondering now if he felt that it would be cheaper to pay someone else to do a job we should've been doing, instead of giving us a $5 dollar allowance as children. Or, if he wanted to give them a job and a couple of dollars in hopes they wouldn't get to stealing anything around the house. Maybe it was both reasons. We always had respect in the hood, I will tell you that. Only one time did we get our bikes stolen after driving on a short trip and leaving them in the driveway unchained. Bikes were the best mode of transportation for the young life before getting our first cars. Your bike was like your horse, an extension of your personality. Pops put the word out in the street that afternoon and we had them back that night; I'll give my dad props for that. I can vividly remember certain individuals stopping by to work, being sober during the entire job, and then seeing them later on at the Burger King up the street, high out of their minds, barely able to recognize me. The demons had seemingly won again. Seeing people that I had compassion for and grew to love, was all the reminder my young self needed to not smoke crack-cocaine, or any illicit synthetic drug. My community experienced a real epidemic, and there was no one to help us or assist us in healing but ourselves. I decided early on that I would not participate in the get-rich-quick money scheme of selling crack to my elders, whom I lovingly referred to as "Auntie and Unc". Nope, I wasn't going to do it. By the time we reached 13-14 years old, many of my friends parents were strung out. Some a little later than others, while most were full-on veteran crack smokers by the time we reached our teens. I am very grateful that my parents never fell victim to those drug-usage ills. There is no way I could look my patnas (partners aka friends) in the eye knowing I just sold their mama a crack rock. Instead, many of my friends whose parents were addicted to dope, would find themselves in the crack game, selling rocks in order to protect their parents, aunties and uncles, and other loved ones who were going to smoke regardless of who sold it to them. My friends all figured that if they didn't sell it, someone else would, and that "someone else" wouldn't have the same compassion towards their parent as they would. I knew if I'd sell it, eventually one of my friends mamas or aunties would approach me without any money, asking for product in exchange for sexual favors, and I just couldn't move myself to have that on my conscience. All of my friends who were really involved in the game appreciated me for that decision I made. It wasn't even about competition; it was about maintaining as much dignity, honor, and respect through a horrible situation as much as humanly possible. The Belly of the Beast is something else.

Most people in wild situations are forced to live a double-life, having to maintain two different narratives of existence. I was one of those rare exceptions that was definitely living a triple-life. One version of my life was the school-boy, doing his best to navigate through the public education system the best way I could, keeping the secrets and reasons close to me as to why I wasn't performing to the highest standard that many of my instructors knew I could. The consequences of not performing well academically in school were that I couldn't join any of the sports teams, which for me, were a source of emotional outlet and stress relief. Then, there was the daily Hood life, where everyone was doing their best to not get caught up in any of the traps set by the city government or ourselves. It was quite difficult to navigate at times because it was almost like the blind leading the blind, with many of the children being the only ones who could see, still not realizing exactly what it was we were looking at. Then, there was the truth about what was taking place behind the four walls of my home. Outside was already perceived to be a hell-hole, where the only glimpse of hope seemed to be us children whose minds were protected as much as angelically possible, enabling us to keep dreaming and hoping for a brighter day. Whenever we played together in those streets, it seemed like all of our troubles went away. So we just kept on playing. But once the street lights turned on in the evening time, and it was time to go inside, that's when many of our realities set in. For me and my siblings, that meant going from the "hell-hole" outside, and deeper into "the pit", that was the inside of our home. Somehow, we were protected. Blinded to the conscience effects of what we were experiencing. We knew our conditions weren't good, but day in and day out, we were just thankful to have a roof over our heads. I think back to those days and I just shake my head. My siblings and I really made it a long way, regardless of the pain and traumas we still deal with internally today. Due to the fact that I couldn't join any of the teams at school for any length of time, I would go up to the church a block from home and hoop in the parking lot for hours. That was my one consistent outlet. Practicing for hours on end every day, working on my handles, my hops, and my shots, really had me thinking that some NBA scout would roll down the street one day, see me hooping, and ask me to tryout for one of the local teams. That one dream kept me from destroying myself. I'm so very thankful for that dream. I never made it onto a championship team, but I won the championship everyday I chose to play hoops on that concrete court, instead of playing in the relentlessly unforgiving and deadly dope game.

By the time I reached nineteen years old, and was out of public school for about two years, I was almost lost. All of the daydreams I'd have about making it to the league, being selected for a college scholarship, making it in boxing, were pretty much out the window. Heck, I didn't even make it to the Marine Corps. I was desperate to figure out what I was going to do, and what I was supposed to do with my life. Imagine not being able to enter into the home you were raised in, with your mother still living there, and you not making your way out of the community that forces you to remember this daily, while being forced to walk past the only place you ever called home. By the time I graduate high school, my life was beginning to spin even more out of control. The reason I kept going to school, and not physically dropping out, is because I'd dedicated so much of my time to it throughout the years, but once I graduated, I didn't have a school building and free food to go to every day.

I was institutionalized. I grew dependent on the system to take care of me. My home life was messy, figuratively and literally. I didn't have access to the resources I needed at home, so I would do my best to get them from school. However, by default, I had to attend school to access the resources. I actually depended on that free breakfast and lunch every day. That was one aspect of my day that I didn't have to worry about while I was at a school; eating food. I grew accustomed to seeing the few people who I considered friends at school. They didn't have to live how I was living so I'd dream through their existence as well. Now, in 2022, it's "cool" to be from the Hood, but when I was coming up, it was an embarrassment and a nightmare, something people would laugh at and ridicule you for. When you were living in the Belly of the Beast, it was common knowledge that you lived as someone who adapted to the pursuits of one who was from the Belly of the Beast; and I fought tooth and nail to avoid living that way. Hence, I always wondered why I lived there in the first place. Once I graduated from high school, and my military enlistment didn't go the way I initially thought it would, I was floating. Myself, along with many of my peers, began living disastrously. I lost many of my patnas to violence, prison and to drugs. One by one, plucked off the branch like a beautiful leaf. All I knew is that I wasn't trying to get plucked off too. So, almost naturally, I began selling pounds of herb to sustain myself financially. The majority of my cannabis sells were to my patnas slanging crack, who wouldn't dare to smoke the hard stuff. I also began taking my music production and song writing seriously. I went to the County Clerks office in Fairfield and filed my first of many fictitious business entities with Brandon, my best friend at the time.

We really thought that we would make it big in the music industry, let me tell you! We had all of the zeal of a young Jay-Z and Dame Dash. We wrote business plans, opened business bank accounts, registered with ASCAP and BMI, and did our absolute best to learn the game. We were promised empty promises that kept us fueled another day. We thought daily on how to raise funds and capital to cover our growing expenses. We even began signing artists to our record label and imprint. We began to get booked for showcases, and whenever someone wouldn't book us, we figured out a way to put our own showcases on, and make them something special. It's crazy, but with all of the initiative and actions we exhibited, the majority of the adults in our lives just sat back and watched, seemingly almost waiting for us to fail. It was like whatever adult-level wisdom they had, they kept to themselves, like we were competition to them, just because we had a dream. Looking back on it all now, we were destined to fail in those seasons of our lives, but no one could've told us that back then.

One day I was on the block shooting dice and cutting up with many of the neighborhood young men, attempting to add a few dollars to my pocket. Usually, if you saw me in a dice game, it was because my financial resources were depleting and I needed a quick come up. When I'm in that frame of mind I always win. On this particular day, we decided to take the "d-game" to an alley located deep inside my hood. Nobody would come where we were unless they were invited, somebody upset mama, or unless they were brave police officers. We always kept our heads on a swivel, and were always quick to dart off if things got funky. Sometimes we could finish a whole game, no hassles, and sometimes we couldn't finish the game due to outside influences halting our game. It always seemed like the best d-games would get stopped prematurely; this would be one of those types of games. As a few of us gathered around the pot of cash, while others looked on in excitement, waiting to see if the person who was on the dice number would hit, we all heard the rollers (police) famous "blurp blurp". We looked up from the dice, and saw two squad cars pulling up. One was at the East end of the alley, and we spotted the other one as we looked through a chain link fence, on the adjacent street from the alley, in the middle of the block, halfway through. It's a universal rule in dice games where if the police show up, or if someone starts shooting, whoever was actively in the game, grabs their money from the pot, and everyone takes off running. We grabbed our loot and got to booking out of the alley in full speed.

I darted out of the alley so fast you'd have thought I was some kin to Usain Bolt. I mean fast. I left everyone. You see, it's every man for themselves when the police get to flexing, and those of us with a weaker mindset, "waiting around to see what's gonna happen", are the ones the police are aiming to capture. It's not easy running through the turf either. The asphalt usually has little pebbles and stones strewn out in random places and one misstep can mean you bite it hard. The alley was located in between Ohio and Louisiana streets. Aunt Sallie's house is on Springs Road. I made it home in no time flat. My mom wasn't there. I ran into the driveway, and made it look as though I'd been there all day, then I walked back out to the street in order to see what the police were doing. On my way running to the house, I remember passing by an elder brother who was manicuring the church on the corner's lawn. He had his work truck parked on my side of the street, so I actually ran right past it as I was making my way home, but I didn't notice it at first. It wasn't until I walked out of my driveway and back up the street to see a few of my friends who had gotten caught by the police, that I took notice of the elder brother and his truck. My friends were forced to sit down on the corner of the church, and have pictures of their face and tattoos taken by the police. The elder brother acted like he wasn't watching what was going on, but he was. He did his best to stay out of it, but if anything got too out of hand as far as police brutality was concerned, he would've definitely stepped in. Once the police seemed like they were wrapping up their "investigation", the elder brother made his way over to me as I stood next to his work truck. He began putting his air blower into the bed of the truck. He then began speaking life to me. It was more like prophecy than anything, as if he knew exactly what was going to happen in my life over the next four years. It was the first time anyone had told me what was going to happen to me. I've always respected my elders and those older than me, even if what they were saying didn't quite make sense; I'd always listen for that one jewel of truth every aged person has to offer. All I could do was listen.

He told me that I would make it in my life. That I was from this place called Millasville, but I wouldn't always be here; that my life was bigger than existing in this Hood. That I was going to make some decisions that would affect the rest of my life, and that once the decisions were made, my life would never be the same. Still, all I could do was listen. I never asked him what these decisions might be. It's like I already knew on a Soul level, even if I couldn't quite articulate the feelings. His words were prophetic. As he was speaking my buddy Brandon, who'd I left to fend for himself, just as I had, finally made his way around the corner, never having witnessed my speed like that before. That was the first day he'd been in the Hood and realized it wasn't all games. He'd also never been left behind by me before. I think I had taught him a valuable lesson that afternoon. As he walked toward me and the elder, the elder slowly began to finish packing up his gear, and told me to be blessed and that God got me. He then concluded his prophetic word with a confirming nod of his head, then didn't speak another word. Brandon finally made it to us, and I got the feeling the elder wanted me to walk away with Brandon, so we made our way back down the street to my house. I saw that elder one more time, about ten minutes later, around the corner from my house on Shasta street as Brandon and I were walking to the Hood liquor store. I never saw the elder again after that.

Everything the elder told me that day came true within four years. He was another Angel.

Bedroom Angel

Some years had passed since the elder had spoken to me. Many things happened to me during the timeframe of me meeting that Angel, and me becoming a husband and father. When I met that elder on the street that fateful day I was 19 years old and the year was the Gregorian Summer of 2004.

The year was now the beginning of Spring 2012. By this time I had been married to my wife for almost four years and we had two sons, ages 3 and 1. We were living in a rented triplex located on Ohio street near the waterfront in Vallejo. We had just arrived home from running errands. I usually get out the car first, taking whatever bags I can, go to open the front door, and make sure everything is copacetic inside before getting the family and leading them inside. This day was no different. Once I got everyone inside, I realized that I was tired. I never lay in my bed with my street clothes on, but this day, I was really in need of a quick rest. I laid down on my side of the bed, not getting under the covers or anything like that, but just stretching out a little. I suppose I could've stretched out on the living room couch, but the children were excited to be home, and were making noise in there. I figured that I wouldn't be going into a full-fledged sleep, so I propped my upper back against the wall with the remainder of my body extended along the edge of the bed. My left leg hanged off the edge with my foot resting on the floor. I'm not sure how long my eyes were closed, but for a split second, I remember achieving REM sleep; it happened so quickly. However, as soon as I reached that state, I heard a voice. It was a whisper. I could literally feel the whisper in my ear; the whisp from the words, the breath, and the vibrations...it made me jump out of my sleep! I opened my eyes and nothing, and I mean nothing, was next to me. I called out to my wife "Babe! Did you hear that?!" She said "no honey, here what?" I told her I had just heard a voice directly in my ear. It sounded like a woman's voice. She just looked at me, checking to see if I was messing with her. When she confirmed the seriousness in my countenance, she stated again that she hadn't heard anything. She asked me what the voice said to me, so I told her. The words that I heard, in a softly angelic, but stern and authoritative voice said to me: "Listen and hear me."

That statement made me jump out of bed. I was not asleep long at all. To this very day I wonder what I am supposed to listen to and hear. That experience felt like an initiation of some sort. As if that was the beginning of many messages which will be delivered to me in that manner. I will never forget those words. I've been patiently awaiting for the next moment when something like that happens to me again.

That was an Angel as well. Honestly, I think that was the Holy Spirit.

Alley Angel

By the summer of 2012 my family and I were living in our own home. I made some sound investment decisions earlier that year which forwarded us the opportunity to leave the triplex near the waterfront and purchase our first property in "Historic Vallejo". During the navy shipyard days of Mare Island, the section of Vallejo we moved to was a neighborhood with homes that were originally built for high ranking military men and their families. So-called Black folks were pretty much prohibited from purchasing property in that area back in those days due to the financial disparities faced by many, but by the time my family and I came along, it was primed for some new, young energy to be infused and moved in. It was a welcomed change for all of us. We were getting pretty "big" in our triplex unit and it was time to leave.

Our new home was a blessing. It was huge. We had four bedrooms, two family rooms, four bathrooms, and two kitchens, a pantry and a laundry room. It was one huge home; not a converted duplex or anything like that.

We knew it was a place where we'd want to raise our growing family and invite our extended family over to have a great time. The remainder of that first year, we focused on settling in and getting our affairs in order, so we pretty much kept to ourselves and did our best to settle into our new home. We made a plan to have our first big get together on the Fourth of July of the next year, 2013, in celebration of my birthday, which took place on July 2nd, and the holiday.

Everyone that we invited was able to make an appearance and it was a huge success. The home was spacious enough to accommodate our large family, and there were plenty of cooked dishes and food grilled on the BBQ for everyone to eat. It was an all day event. By the time the evening came, everyone began trying to figure out where we'd watch the fireworks. Would we all go down to the waterfront a short distance walk down the street, or would we stay at our home and stand on the porch to watch them? Those were the most popular options. We unanimously chose to view the festivities from the porch. Those who opted to view the fireworks from the waterfront, drove to the waterfront and viewed them from there, and then made their way back to our home.

I decided to stay at home because I was still cooking some meat on the grill, and I hadn't eaten all day. I figured that I'd finish cooking and make myself a plate to eat while the family was outside watching the fireworks.

My wife, mother, and my wife's auntie, were wrapping food up in the kitchen when I playfully said "y'all make sure to save me somethin' to eat nah", and then asked if they can put me a plate together as I headed out back to finish grilling the meat. As I made my way to the backyard, I checked the condition of our family area downstairs, ensuring that everyone had actually migrated to either of the agreed upon destinations for where fireworks would be viewed. I didn't see anyone downstairs so I walked outside towards the grill. The beef ribs were doing phenomenally in the rib-rack that belonged to my auntie. She was kind enough to allow me to use it that day, seeing how much meat I was going to have to cook. As I opened the lid to the grill, a huge waft of BBQ smoke billowed up and into the slight evening breeze. I always use the best combination of seasonings when I cook, and this occasion would be no different. The meat was tender, succulent, and well-seasoned. I like to grill meat so that no BBQ sauce is needed. I'll use BBQ sauce, but only as an addition, not a cover-up for lack of seasoning or poor grilling technique. As I closed the grill lid, I decided I'd step through the garage door and into the alley that was situated directly behind our house. With the garage door raised, I made my way back to the alley to see if I could possibly spot the fireworks being ignited at the waterfront. I couldn't see any sparkling colors emanating in the sky, but I could hear the blasts in the distance. I was facing west, towards the farthest end of the alley from our home. Our home was situated right in front of the only light pole in the entire alley on our block, so I dubbed our residence "Lighthouse" because it was essentially the middle-point as people made their way up and down the alley daily. As I was facing the west, I felt a sense to turn around; someone or something was close by. The feeling is what I'd guess Spider-Man's "spidey sense" feels like whenever he realizes something is near to him that requires his attention. In the shadows, along the eastern entrance of the alley, I saw a figure of a man, at the edge of the entrance into our section of the alley, take a step off of the sidewalk and into the alley, walking towards my direction. I remained looking towards his direction because I wanted to see if I could recognize who he was. Many people used the alley as a shortcut to get to the other side of the block quickly, so perhaps he was doing the same, and was passing by. As he got closer to me, I realized that I hadn't seen this guy before. His hair was dark brown, and it was flowing, but was cut to around the middle of his neck, not quite shoulder length. He appeared to be a Caucasian man. It was the beginning of July but he wore a zipped black leather jacket, black jeans, and had on black boots. All that he appeared to be missing was his loud, custom Harley-Davidson. He made his way down the alley and by default, had to come near me because I hadn't moved from my position. I spoke first and asked him how he was doing this "fine evening". He replied that he was doing well now that he had seen me. I found it kind of strange, but took the statement as "he'd been walking some time before he'd seen anyone that evening, and was grateful that I'd initiated the conversation." He stopped in front of me and began talking. He asked how I was doing and if I was cooking for the Fourth. I told I was feeling great and that I was actually cooking to celebrate my birthday, but we were recognizing it on the Fourth so that family and friends could swing by and kick it with us for the day. He told me happy birthday and I of course replied with a thank you. Whenever I meet someone, I do my best to make them feel welcome and comfortable; as if we'd known each for years. I asked him what he was doing in the area and he told me that he was just passing through and smelled the meat grilling. He said he could smell it from way on the other side of the block. I appreciated the comment. I then asked him what it was he did for work. He told that he was currently staying at a shelter, assisting the head Pastor with day to day operations. Without me telling him what my interests were or what it was that I did for a living, he then told me that I was a musician. He then made a statement that I will never forget. He said "…and Everyone knows who you are." I looked at him in bewilderment, but for some reason I couldn't reply to ask him "well how did you know I record music, and what do you mean 'Everyone knows who I am?'" He made the statement again, as matter-of-factly as the first time, "Everyone knows who you are". At that moment, all I could do was ask him if he'd like a plate to eat. Now mind you, I hadn't eaten yet at all. Everyone at the party had eaten, so I knew whatever food was left, there had to be enough at least for one more guest plate. He replied that he'd indeed like a plate, but also mentioned a woman and her two young children who were staying at the shelter. He humbly asked if I could make them something to eat, and that he was sure they'd greatly appreciate it. I quickly responded with a "yes, I can make them something to eat as well." He was very grateful. I told him to please wait in the alley, and I'd be right back out with some food.

Once I began making my way back inside, I slightly turned around to make sure that he wasn't following in behind me. Even though I felt an immediate sense to help him, I'd just met this man, and wasn't quite sure if he'd respect my request for him to stay in the alley while I went inside. I opened the sliding door to the downstairs family area, and as I closed it shut, sure enough, the man was standing by the light pole. I was grateful he was following my instructions.

I made my up the stairs to the third level of our home, and then down the stairs, and into the kitchen area. My mother and auntie were still in the kitchen when my wife, perfectly timing herself, walked into the kitchen from the front of the house where everybody else was standing watching fireworks. She immediately reminded me to eat something. I said "ok babe." That is also when I asked everyone if there was enough food to make some more plates. They were kind of stupefied, partly because they hadn't yet made my plate of dinner for me to eat, but also because they'd spent the last fifteen

minutes or so, in the process of packing everything up for refrigeration. I
told them that there was a gentleman in the alley that I'd just met, who was
on his way back to the home-transition shelter when he stopped and began
chatting with me. I told them that he had made me aware of a mother and her
two young children that would be extremely grateful if I'd give them some
food to eat. My wife, mother, and auntie agreed that I should give the man
some food, so I kindly instructed them to place every variety of food we had
that evening onto plates. I asked them to separate the food by the type it was
so that nothing would be messy, and so that when the family received the
food, the mother could ration the food out to her children how she felt fit.
The plates were made: ribs, chicken, and hotdogs on a few plates, salads on
another couple plates, sides on a couple plates, and buns, rolls, and cornbread
on the remaining plates. They also put the man a plate together for himself.
Once the plates were packed into grocery bags, I headed back downstairs
and out the house towards the alley. It had been about ten minutes, and I
was hoping that I wouldn't be surprised by the man standing in my garage,
or by him snooping around. What I saw next was just as astonishing as him
stating that "Everyone knew who I was." I walked out my garage and into the
alley. At the very moment I step into the alley, I noticed the man wasn't in the
area where I'd last seen him facing the eastern entrance of the alley. Looking
towards the direction of where he might be, I swiveled towards the western
entrance of the alley because I also heard a vehicle entering. There the man
was, sitting on the concrete, "Indian-style", as if meditating. He was there
the entire time I'd went back inside, waiting patiently on my return. All of
my thoughts about if he had been snooping around immediately dissipated.
I had never witnessed anything like that before. He remained seated as the
vehicle approached. I recognized the vehicle as my younger brother Justin's
car. He, our sister, and her boyfriend had made it back to my home from
the waterfront. As my brother got closer to where he had originally parked
before pulling off to go to the waterfront, he honked at the sitting man as if
the man was some sort of animal in the middle of the road. I was immediately
disappointed, and embarrassed by Justin's actions. I quickly apologized to
the man for my brother's behavior. The man told me gently that it was okay,

and he got up and came towards me. My brother, sister, and her boyfriend got out of the car and were acting very unusual. They were timid concerning this man, but were acting as if they weren't. I had to motion for them to walk by us and go inside, and that I'd be inside to get with them soon. As I handed the man the bagged plates of food, my brother made a disparaging remark towards the man, for which I had to apologize again. Once they were inside I explained how the plates were bagged; where his plate was located and where the mother and her children's plates were located. I spoke blessings to the man, and told him to enjoy his food and to have safe travels. He told me that I would always be blessed, and that "they were proud of me." I still didn't ask him who "Everyone" and "They" were; I was too concerned about he, the hungry mother, and her children's welfare to ask about the initial statement, and too frazzled by my brother's actions to even consider asking the man about the "they" comment. We said our goodbyes, and I watchfully saw him out of the alley. I'd never see him again. I prayed that he would make it safely back to the shelter and that there would be enough for those who needed food to eat. I immediately felt like everything would be just fine.

It was at that moment, once he was out of my sight, that I realized something miraculous had just occurred. I felt as though I was Abraham, tending to the Angels who visited he and Sarah many millennia ago.

Yes, something miraculous had indeed happened.

Even though I'm a so-called Black man, and there is so much racial tension in the nation, I never treat people badly. Regardless of another persons ethnicity, I treat them as a brother and a sister. My mom always reminded me throughout my life to treat people with kindness because I may be "speaking with an Angel, unaware of who I'm actually talking to." Angels will come to us to test our hearts. They will come in many different ethnic identities, oftentimes in a different form than what we are used to or expecting in order to test the true kindness of our Souls. Some of us pass the test. Sadly, many of us don't pass the test.

I had just spoken with and provided sustenance to an Angel. I truly *was* blessed.

"Willie Jean Thompson"

My neighbor Al had recently moved and relocated out of the Bay Area. It was a pretty strenuous move for him, but he gathered up the strength needed to make it happen. There are always loose-ends that need to be tied when making a move of any magnitude, let alone a move out of the state. When he finally touched down in his new location and began to get settled in, he text messaged me and asked if I could go next door to his house and collect the mail that hadn't been redirected to his new address. I gladly fulfilled his request and grabbed his mail. He'd collected many pieces since his departure, and a new tenant had moved in, assisting me in retrieving his mail that was inside of the home.

It was requested by Al that I send him his mail, boxed up, through the Post Office. I told him to give me a couple days to make it happen because I was working on another project that needed my attention at home.

When time came for me to go to the Post Office and send him his mail, I'd decided to visit the small, recently opened branch in downtown Vallejo. I drove by the location to make sure they were opened, then I flipped a u-turn and found a parking spot on the corner, The Empress Theatre behind me. As I pulled up, I noticed a little, elder woman, sitting on the edge of one of those raised cement garden beds normally in front of buildings located in downtown and business districts of cities.

I parked my truck. I then glanced over to my passenger seat to make sure that my package was sealed correctly and ready to be shipped out. After confirming that the package was good to go, I looked to my left to see the little elder woman, still sitting in the place she'd been sitting when I first pulled. Whenever people are standing or sitting down in front of a building I'm going to have to walk into, I brace myself because I know and innately feel that I will be speaking to them in some capacity. A quick "Hi, how are you today?" turns into a long therapy session where an entire life-story is shared with me. Ok, most of the time it's just a specific season of life the person wants to share with me, but those are usually some long seasons! When I asked the little elder woman how she was doing, she smiled at me and told me how mannerable I was. "Mannerable" is a word in my community. I recognized the light within this little elder woman, but something was amiss, so I told her that as soon as I was done handling the shipment of the package I had in my hands, that I'd be back outside to chat with her. I asked her not to go anywhere and wait for me to return.

I was raised to respect and honor my elders. I suppose that "respect and honor" is one reason it took me so long to write this book. I had to make sure that when I wrote it, I wouldn't smudge the facts, but also deliver them in the most honorable and respectful manner possible in regards to my earth parents. Many people reading this story might disagree with this approach, but they have their own stories to tell. The experiences I faced as a child, teenager, and young adult, were many of the same seasons being played out over and over again, similar to the film Groundhog Day starring Bill Murray. What was the Most High Mama & Papa trying to teach me? I was being primed for placement into the eventual position to help and assist many through their most traumatic life experiences. I was being conditioned to keep a warm heart, and to maintain that child-like innocence into my adulthood so that I could be of service to the masses. That intense curiosity and inquisitiveness blessed to me as a child, would came in handy as an adult, if I could only shield myself from the ills of the people in the world long enough to not form a callous and cold heart, losing that innocence that kept me as pure as humanly possible.

When I was done with my task inside the Post Office, I made me way back outside and over to the little elder woman. By this time she was riled up about something, cussing at some people who I'd later find out had been harassing her. I knew that I had to calm her down so I quickly made my way over to her as she remained seated on the raised cement flower bed. I stayed standing for the moment because I had to ensure there were no immediate threats around us. That's when I asked her what had happened. "Them fu**ers over there keep on messing with me!", she said. "God don't like ugly and He ain't too fond of pretty either!" I nodded my head in agreement and said "you right Mama". I told you, this is about respect. When a woman from my community appears to be my mothers age I call her "Auntie". When a woman appears to be one of my grandmothers ages I call her "Mama". She fit into the latter age group, so "Mama" it was.

She had gotten up from where she was seated by this time, and paced a few steps towards the intersection corner, so I made my way closer to her to see who she was talking about. I could see a group of three hipsters communing in front of an art gallery store that had been recently renovated and opened across the street from where we were standing. Vallejo had, in recent years, gone through an overhaul of sorts, with all kinds of techy and hipster types relocating into the area from San Francisco and from other parts of the Bay, as well as the nation, bringing with them a ton of expectant, snobby energy and demands that weren't really in line with the spirit of the areas they moved in to. If they weren't trying their hand in entrepreneurialism, they caught the ferry to San Francisco to work at one of the startups or already established tech companies. Many of them purchased homes in the area. Most of them were late seventies and early eighties babies. They called themselves renovating what they believed to an abandoned downtown district. They clearly weren't aware of the history of downtown Vallejo and what made it appear to be dilapidated. They were the uppity type and I could immediately sense that had I not stood next to Mama, they would've managed to harass and threaten her some more. I could tell my presence made her tough and ready to take them all on; I was her young, strong and tall, hair wrapped, beard in locks, Black super hero come to save the day. Her special security guard. Once she settled down for a moment, we began to chat. She explained how they didn't respect her for sitting where she was, for how long she was sitting. She told me that she lived down the street and that she needed some fresh air because it was too hot in her apartment. This little elder wasn't hurting anybody. She was physically all alone by the time I'd come up. By the time she calmed down, the hipsters left the scene and we could really get to the nitty gritty of things.

She was impressed with my kindness and my willingness to spend a few moments of my time with her. I motioned to her to sit down again. We immediately got comfortable with each other. Her energy felt kindred, and I'm sure she'd tell you the same about mine. So much so, I felt as though I really was speaking with one of my grandmothers. I wasn't about to let anything but goodness happen to this elder. She began mentioning to me how she wasn't perfect, and that she'd made some mistakes in life. She told me that she had children but none of them wanted anything to do with her. I was telling myself in my mind that "I have to speak life to this elder. I have to let her know that she was perfectly made, living her unique experience as the eyes and ears of the Most High Mama&Papa through her avatar." She continued her testimony, and that I could do was look at her and listen in amazement. She come a mighty long way. She noticed the peace covering me, so naturally, she began to cry. All I could do at this point was gently place my long arm around her shoulder and listen to her. She continued on with saying how she'd abused drugs over the years and that she never brought nobody down with her. She was as responsible as she could be, kept her own place, and minded her business. She began to stop crying as I held her close, just as a loving and understanding son would do for his emotionally inflicted mother. I told her how she was perfect. How she was the only one on this earth who could've gotten as far in the life she was leading as she did, because her experience up to that point was specifically tailored for her by The Most High. She just looked at me and called me an Angel. She then asked me, dried eyes and teary sniffles gone: "do you believe in Jesus?" I told her yes mam. She said "you really ARE an Angel, then she slapped her thigh lightly in exclamation. The way she asked that question though…it made me feel as though I was being tested. One thing I learned about religion over the years, is that it's best policy to meet people where they are in their journey, instead of trying to "elevate" them to where you are in yours. I refer to "Jesus" as Yahushua now, but that doesn't remove me from the fact that during the majority of my life I knew Him as "Jesus".

The little elder was so excited by my answer. She then told me her name: Willie Jean Thompson. She was originally from North Carolina and had made her way to Vallejo way back in the fifties when her family relocated. As we were talking, a few people passing by from the neighborhood noticed the attention I was giving her, and was proud at what they saw. One brother was walking down the street with groceries and threw up the Black Power fist, a universal gesture of gratitude and appreciation between Brothas, as he waited for the light to turn green so he could cross the street.

Mama Willie Jean was so thrilled and her day literally turned around. I told her I'd check on her whenever I was in the area, and that she was "blessed by the best, and to pretty to stress." She was happy. We prayed together, and then she all but skipped off towards her home, and I watched her a few moments longer before getting into my truck. I gave thanks to The Most High Mama & Papa for the blessed encounter, and then I started my truck, backed out of parking space, and pulled off.

The next couple days I drove past that location, and around the area where I saw her walking towards after our conversation. There was no sign of her anywhere. Over the next couple weeks or so I made it a point to drive down that way, just catch a glimpse of her sitting on the edge of that raise cement flower bed, and still, no Mama.

I was already feeling it, that familiar feeling when something supernatural had occurred. I couldn't chalk up as anything but an encounter with another Angel.

I had never seen her again, but I knew who she really was:

Mama "Willie Jean Thompson" was an Angel in disguise as an elder woman sent to test a Son of God to see whose side I was really on. She was also the only Angel I had encountered up to that point, who'd given me a name to reference.

I'm thrilled to report to you that I passed that test exam with flying colors.

I know it's difficult to navigate through a world of people that are asleep, and the loneliness that one can feel at times. Yes it is hard. I'm an empath, amongst many other things, so there is often a sense of sadness that comes over me for the majority of the people of the world. Storing pertinent information in my mind and dispensing it to those who would give me a window of opportunity to share is what lightens the emotional load for me. What keeps me from going crazy is the amount of gratitude I express daily, recognizing that this sharing of information is one of the callings on my life. I give thanks always, and I speak with Nature always.

When I was a little boy, I was confronted with a choice: pray for earthly riches or pray for wisdom. I chose wisdom. All things earthly riches cannot buy have been added unto me. Wisdom has even added material riches unto me. Wisdom is what should be sought after. With Sound Wisdom, which is the correct use of right knowledge, you will continue to go far in life. With the covering of light and love over you, the overwhelming feelings of revelation and truth being exposed won't seem so much as a burden. It's time to begin sharing what you've learned. Don't hide or dim your light. Those meant to resonate with you will. I don't go crazy because I Am a vessel of Truth. The Truth will always be liberating. Blessings of light and love to you always. You got this!
Stay Vigilant.

5

"I Believe I Can Fly"

"*Remember to keep yourself alive, there is nothing more important than that.*"
     -Afeni Shakur

I grew up.

I wish I knew my destiny back then, but all I wanted to do was make someone happy with me. Anyone honestly.

Life was always fun. Life was always beautiful. I was always affectionate and caring. It wasn't until later in my life that I realized the level of empathy I held for those whose path I had crossed; I always just thought I cared too much and should mind my business.

I never realized that I was feeling so many others feelings and emotions, that I'd somehow taken them onto myself, living them, breathing them, entrenched in them. Always to the point that the one who shared those feelings with me left the scene feeling lighter while I somehow had to bare a load that seemed heavy as a ton; even for my small childish frame. When did I become the adult, having to manage everyone's emotions, while all the adults had

81

seemingly become children? Was I chosen to experience this or did I choose, in some far off past-life, to not only embrace this destiny, but also create it for myself? What was the lesson I was to learn?

Confusion is an illusion.

There is no need to be confused once we grasp the idea that everything happens for a reason. There are truly no coincidences in our lives, only synchronicities. When we realize that our individual experiences are meant to serve us, and meant to make us aware of what our true purpose in life actually is, we will begin to look at our journey differently, and in a more positive light.

The perspective I hold day by day, does not, and should not, be the same perspective you hold day by day. The idea that you and I must see life the same begins in childhood, when all we want to do is make friends and be in harmony with those we are surrounded by. Think about.

When we began daycare or school for the first time and was led down the hallway to enter into our new classroom, with everyone stopping what they were doing to look up at you walking through the door, did you know what to expect? I knew that if I could identify at least one person who was doing something that I could relate to, that I would go over to them, introduce myself, and ask if I could join in on the fun. There would always be a few groups of children doing what children do, but only one or two of the groups would actually resonate with me to the point of me wanting to join in and participate. Being anxious and a little nervous would definitely keep me from attempting to join the groups I didn't feel comfortable with because they weren't doing anything I could relate to. Right?

Well, the truth is, that just because we saw a group of children doing what we liked to do, it wasn't a guarantee that we'd be invited to join in the activity because those children might've already had their active number of participants figured out and one more player would be one too many. Or maybe, that particular group of children wasn't kind, so when you walked up to the table and asked if you could join in, they immediately shut you down, even though you resonated with what they were doing. You had failed to realize that you might not resonate with the actual group of children that you chose to connect with.

It was at this point that, instead of going to your assigned seat and sitting alone, you decided to go over to one of the groups participating in an activity that you did not resonate with. You soon realized that you truly resonated with the actual people in the group more-so than the activity they were engaged in. This is also when you began to realize that you had the capacity and capability to expand your thinking to learn a new thing, even if what you decided to learn didn't initially resonate with you.

The relief we feel when our presence is wanted and appreciated can be exhilarating and totally life-changing. To not feel like an outcast is so important in our primary years of existence. Many of us, especially early on in life, don't realize the effects our treatment of others will have on them, not only in that present moment, but well into the future. We fail to realize how powerful, harmful, and impactful, our distasteful actions can be, if not corrected and accounted for as soon as possible.

Did you know that people question themselves all the time? Self-worth is the opinion we have of ourselves and the value we place onto ourselves. It's essentially how we see ourselves at any given moment, and we are always questioning whether or not we are valued in the eyes of another, whether we realize it or not. If we believe, know, and feel, that we are good people who deserve the best this life has to offer, our potential to bypass what others believe and feel about us can be ignored. When we arrive at the juncture in life where none of our attention or energy is given to such debilitating viewpoints as being worthless in the eyes of another, we can then begin focusing on those qualities about ourselves that make us unique and more than worthy of our existence.

Every generation on earth has had its own era-defining genre of music that helped to inspire, guide and push it through to the next level of attainment and generational success. My era was defined by Hip-Hop, Rap, and R&B.

As a little boy, I craved the deep, pounding bass-lines and crisp snare drum hits sounding like large groups of synchronized claps that Hip-Hop producers were known to create. We called these sounds "knock" or "slap" in my Hood. All throughout the day and well into the night, I could hear the sounds of Rap music playing on someone's sound-system, vibrating from huge speakers located in the trunk of their vehicle. Depending on whose car it was, and the time of day, I could hear smooth melodic bass lines and rhythms filling the air, accompanied by sultry voices in the form of the latest and freshest R&B music.

I've always been a musician; I was born one. I received a Playskool Saxophone when I was about two and a half years old, and taught myself how to play "Twinkle Twinkle Little Star" on it. My earliest music hero's and influences were Cab Calloway and Ray Charles. After seeing these two guys perform on the hit children series Sesame Street, as well as on film in the movie The Blues Brothers starring Dan Aykroyd and John Belushi, I knew that the life of a musician was for me. There were a couple of music stores on Webster street in Alameda CA, where we lived at the time, and I'd always beg my mom to get me a real saxophone. They'd be hanging up in the storefront windows as we'd walk by, and I couldn't help but feel the magnetic attraction to those beautifully designed instruments. It's funny how life works, but I never did get that saxophone. Perhaps I will one day.

It's kind of ironic, but growing up in the Hood in the Millasville section of Central Vallejo CA, around all of the different energy, sounds, and daily pursuits one might witness, I wasn't allowed to listen to Rap music at all. Now, there were a couple of acts, like MC Hammer, a Bay Area Oakland native, and

Will Smith aka The Fresh Prince, who had "cleaner" lyrics that I was able to listen to occasionally, but for the most part, I was raised on Solid Gold Soul, the Blues, and Gospel music. I had to sneak the types of Rap music I really wanted to listen to, with my first official mixtape being a conglomeration of Snoop Doggy Dog, Warren G and Nate Dogg hits; G-Funk is what they called it. My first official tape (yes, back then we listened to our music on cassette tapes) was "Nuthin' But A G Thang", the radio edit, by Dr. Dre and Snoop Dogg. I received the tape as a gift from one of my aunties after shopping around the mall with her. My brother, who is two years younger than me, was also given his first Rap cassette tape that day as well, and I'm not going to lie, I was kind of salty about that, not because he received something too, but because his tape was an original cut and wasn't edited for foul language!

Back in the early nineties, Snoop Doggy Dogg's music was the "hottest thing smoking". I listened to that song "Nuthin' But A G Thang" all day, every day, and twice on Sundays as a seven year old. Everyone in the neighborhood was playing it too, keeping it in heavy rotation, so one could literally hear it being played everywhere. By the time summer was over and I got back to school to begin the second grade, I'd mastered the flow, and had everybody in my class buzzin' about how dope I could rap that song. When it was time to get to that part of the lyrics where Snoop would spell out his name, I'd hit it on point every single time! It's a trip, but I don't remember ever having stage fright.

A year later I'd be massively influenced and grateful for a new sound from five young brothas coming out of Cleveland Ohio, named Bone-Thugs-In-Harmony. The very first of their songs that I heard was "First of the Month", an instant classic and one of the groups mega-hits. Now it was time to learn a new flow, but I still wasn't allowed to listen to Rap...so I had to sneak around with their tapes too.

During this same time in Pop Culture, Michael Jordan was taking the game of basketball to all new heights and was at the cusp of his Chicago Bulls team's first Three-peat Championship run. Tupac Shakur had recently been released from prison for a crime he didn't commit, and signed a recording deal with Death Row Records. Also during this time, R. Kelly, the greatest song-writer of his generation, was also rising in the ranks of the music world as a multi-platinum R&B artist, writing and producing songs for the likes of Michael Jackson, as well as for many other well-established musical acts that preceded him. R. Kelly has always been a true force to reckon with.

We all wanted to be like Mike. That might might be an understatement.

I always found it ironic how three of the worlds top performing artists were name Michael and two of the three had the same exact initials (MJJ). We had Michael Joseph Jackson, Michael Jeffrey Jordan, and Michael Gerard Tyson. Choose one; whoever you chose, you weren't going to lose!

The "Mike" we really wanted to be like though was Mike Jordan. Actually, I think at different sectors of the season, who we really wanted to be depended on how we were feeling. If it was wet outside we definitely wanted to be Michael Jackson so we could moonwalk on all of the crosswalk paint. If it was time to throw them hands, regardless of the weather, we were channeling Mike Tyson's Punch-out. Every child in every hood either wanted to knock you out like "Iron" Mike, dance you under the table like Michael Jackson, or dunk on your head like MJ. Like I said, whoever you chose, you weren't going to lose!

1996 was crazy year. Michael Jordan and the Chicago Bulls defeated Oakland Native Gary Payton and the Seattle SuperSonics in six games to win the NBA Championship. Tupac Shakur was violently gunned down on the strip in Las Vegas after attending Mike Tyson's championship fight against Bruce Seldon. "Iron" Mike would go on to win the championship in 1:49. Tupac would transition on September 13, 1996 at University Medical Center of Southern Nevada. Oh, and I began the sixth grade.

After winning his fourth NBA championship, Michael Jordan would star in the box-office smash Space Jam later that year, and R. Kelly would release the soon-to-be all-time greatest hit on the Space Jam soundtrack "I Believe I Can Fly". Both R. Kelly and Michael Jordan represented Chi-Town heavy in 1996.

The loss of Tupac was absolutely tragic. It affected me deeply. I was in the sixth grade when Pac dropped "The Don Killuminati: The 7 Day Theory", and it was an instant success. Partly because it was literally slappin', and partly because it was the first album release after his death. Listening to Tupac was a rite of passage. If you weren't up on the metaphors Pac was dropping you were considered a real "L7"…that's a square.

In my Hood where I grew up, the telephone poles from the corner of Shasta street up to 704 Springs Road, were the boundaries I could not cross, and if I made my way past either one by even a molecule, I'd be in big trouble! Our Hood was a hub for every activity you can think of. It was real tribal too. Most of the adults knew you either by face or by "hey Lil (whoever your parent they knew) name."

This might sound funny or strange depending on your upbringing, but I was so happy when sagging became popular. I was one of those little boys who had to sag his pants most days. I only sagged my pants because my pants were always flooding at the ankles. Whenever I sagged my pants, I'd tie my sweatshirt around my waste to make it look like I actually wasn't sagging.

My mom and dad were pretty conservative when it came to spending money on the clothes I needed. My dad liked to keep his money for the things he wanted to do. For school shopping, once a year, every summer, he'd literally give my mom $50 for my brother and I to get school clothes. Not $50 a piece; $50 period. My mom would make it stretch by adding some of her work/medical leave pay from the University, but that even came with a catch. We had to shop for my clothes at the thrift store and the goodwill. I did my absolute best not to ever complain, and hoped every time before parking the car, let alone walking inside, that nobody from school saw me. It took me a couple years to realize that if someone from school saw me inside at the goodwill, they were probably in the same boat as me, so it'd be our secret come school time that we both got our clothes from there.

The majority of my clothes were little man clothes. Dockers and khaki slacks that fit too well at the store, so by the time my mom washed them, they shrunk. Button up plaid collared shirts that did the same thing. It was either that or nothing; and I was going to school whether I wanted to or not. I had to learn how to be cool from the inside out, not from the outside in. Even though the gift remained with me always, I didn't realize the value of such a gift as self-worth, until I got a lot older.

When it came to shoes, we'd get those from Payless Shoe Source. Oh the agony. Once again, I'd do my absolute best not to complain. Those shoes always had un-cushioned soles, and they didn't last too long. I'd do my absolute best to keep them clean too; we'd only get one pair of shoes for the entire year, and maybe a pair of church shoes, but that was only if we outgrew the previous pair! I couldn't tell you how many times I had a pair of shoes with holes in the bottom, or a hole/rip along the sides by the toe area after wearing them everyday for a month straight.

Shoes and clothes didn't really "matter" from kindergarten to about 3rd grade, but once 4th grade hit, folks would take notice if you weren't styling at school. Children start to play harder at that age too. Certain resources are necessary when coming up as a child. I would ask my mom, "please mom, will you get me some Nikes, it doesn't really matter which ones", because I knew that Nikes were made a little better than $19.99 Payless shoes. The only place I knew where we could possibly purchase Nike shoes was Mr. Cools in Vallejo Plaza. She wasn't going to buy me anything from there because they marked everything up. I didn't find out about the Nike store until about the 9th grade. I didn't even know where to buy the cool clothes.

Technically, I had my first pair of Nikes when I was one year old. They were

Nike Cortez baby shoes. I didn't get my first pair of large-sized Nikes from Big 5 until the 8th grade. The reason I keep bringing up "Nike" is because once the 4th grade hit, if you didn't have a pair of Fila, Reebok, Air Jordan's, or Nike brand shoes, the potential for you to get capped on, sigged on, or johnied on, aka roasted, was pretty high. As we all know I'm sure, children at times, can be the meanest people on earth. I would watch children come back to school from Christmas vacation with all sorts of new outfits and shoes ordered fresh from the Eastbay magazine. I always congratulated my folks, never did I envy them, I just wondered when the time would come where I'd get my chance to get cool clothes and kicks. When when two-time NBA Champion and back-to-back finals MVP Hakeem Olajuwon dropped his black and white patent leather #34's at Payless in 1995, I must say I was excited. Finally, a dope shoe at Payless by someone who knew what it was like to have large-sized feet. The patent leather variation flew off the shelves; they were a real hit. Ese gan oooo (Thank you) Hakeem! Asé

One afternoon in 1994, while we were all in the street playing, a car started rolling towards us from the Burger King direction. It was a beautiful sunny summer afternoon and the street was ours. We didn't have any school, and we could play outside all day if we wanted. As the car rolled up, we couldn't tell who was in it, but it was rolling kind of fast, it had two passengers inside of it, and the music was knockin'. As the car got closer we could barely make out who it was. We'd know who it was if we recognized the car cause it's the Hood. This was a car type we'd seen before, a Honda Civic, but the people inside we had never seen. As the car got closer to us while were still playing in the street, all we could hear was a loud strong voice that definitely sounded like it belonged in the Hood with us. It said "Get out the street lil ni**as!" And then we heard a trademark laugh and finally recognized who it was. It was Tupac Shakur, riding in the passenger side of the car, bobbing up and down in his seat being moved by music he and the driver was listening to, while at the same time messing with us. Myself and another little boy excitedly said "Hey y'all, that's Tupac!!!", so we all rushed the car while it was at the stop sign, but before we could reach the car, the driver skirted off down the street. That was first and only time seeing Tupac alive and in the flesh. We were tooooo juiced that day. When he was shot about two years later in Las Vegas, we all listened to updates on his condition via the radio. We were outside on the same street playing the day Chuy Gomez reported that Tupac had succumbed to his wounds and passed away. We were all sad that day. Game over.

When I got towards the end of the 5th grade, I'd heard that Michael Jordan was going to star in a cartoon movie named Space Jam. It was billed as the sportsman's *Who Framed Roger Rabbit.* Everyone was excited. By the time 1996 rolled around we were ready to go see it at the movies.

My living conditions were beginning to be unbearable, but it was like a "slow progression" into what it would eventually become, so instead of being hit by the clutter and hoarding all at once, it was gradual. In 1996, we started to reach a hoarding peak. I didn't know what motivation was during those days, but I sure was looking for it. The film Space Jam was released and did super good in theaters. I had to wait for it to hit VHS tape. The soundtrack was amazing but there was one song in the film that would stick out to me the most. That song is, and was, "I Believe I Can Fly" written and performed by R. Kelly. That one song captured everything I was feeling at that point in my life and gave me the hope I needed to keep going. It became my theme-song. My super-hero music. It was also the song chosen for my 6th grade promotion.

I taught myself how to play basketball. Most of my games were played in the driveway at home, the school basketball courts, or up the street at the church. Our home hoop was made from a wide piece of plywood, and a modified plastic Playskool basketball hoop. We even had a net for it. I would model myself after players like MJ, Grant Hill, and a new young Rookie fresh out of High School named Kobe Bryant. I started dunking the ball by the 7th grade, and was feeling very good about myself. I thought I was going to make it to the NBA just because I could dunk. Hahaha.

The scene got tricky in Junior high school. If you were a child in financial constraints like I was, and you didn't like being the butt of everyone's jokes, and you were a risk-taker, people had better watch out. In the boys locker room during physical education, many lockers would be broken into. I was friends with all of the thieves. We were the ones who couldn't afford the Lugz boots or the Reggie Miller's, so if a cocky or snooty young fella was bumping off at the gums, someone of less fortunate means would break into his locker and take his shoes. We'd often return from the hoop courts into the locker room to see pried opened lockers throughout. Those snooty ones would usually shut up. Some would try to fight but the thief would already be halfway home by the time the end-of-period bell rang.

Holes in my shoes and rips in the crotch of my pants because I was growing so fast. Just sitting down in some of my classes was embarrassing because the teacher would have us sitting across from one another. I usually placed my sweatshirt over my groin area so I wouldn't accidentally expose myself, but some days, I wouldn't even realize I had a hole in the crotch until class was well underway.

I eventually grew to the height of 6'6" just like Mike and Kobe.

I had multiple growth spurts throughout childhood into adulthood. I remember my constant growth as being the excuse my mom would use for not getting me new clothes for me, and the reason why she would get my shoes from Payless. Her theory was "I was just going to grow out of them anyway." She didn't understand the pressures I faced daily at school to fit in. At school, the only thing I'd really attend for is the food. I truly depended on those free school meals daily for sustenance. I had a few new friends too.

Most of my cool clothes came from my Aunt Kathy, who worked at Levi Strauss's corporate office, as well as her and my mom's younger sister, My Auntie Elaine. Aunt Kathy's clothes gift would be brand new, the only catch was, they were promo pieces. That means that they would be new, but maybe a button was missing, or maybe some other element was missing or in a strange place and they would definitely shrink once washed. This meant that I had to wear them as soon as I received them. Auntie Elaine would come to my house towards the end of the summer and drop off a black Glad bag of her sons clothes from a couple years prior. He always had the name brand clothing so whatever I received in that bag I cherished with all my heart. Even though the pants would be big in the waist, and the shirts might be little large, the length was usually there so I figured out a way to keep them up.

Once I got too the 10th grade I started to figure out my own style. For instance, I would color my Nike logos with highlighter markers to match my fit (outfit) for the day. After I did this a few times, folks began to take notice. I never do things for people to take notice though. I do things because they make me feel comfortable. The summer going into the 10th grade was also the year my parents split up for a while.

During these years I was ridiculed heavy at school. All of sudden I'd gone from being picked first in elementary school to not being picked for sports games first, and instead picked last. I'd have to walk 1.4 miles to school and back home for many days while my parents were at home doing whatever it was they'd be doing. I had to do all of this without complaining. It's only now, that I'm a parent myself, where I realize that things could've been done differently. However, as an awakened Soul, I realize that things had to be just as they were.

It's funny, after all these years: I still believe I can fly. Correction. **Now I know I can fly.**

6

"One of Nineteen. Wowzers!"

Ever since I was a little boy, and first could walk and talk, my dad had been open with my brother Justin and I about our older siblings who lived in Chicago. When our big brother Teeter came to live with us in Alameda I was about 3 years old. Teeter was the baby of the Chicago bunch, or at least that's what was presented and told to us by our dad.

Growing up, I was always inquisitive about his children. Always asking how they were, what were their names, how old they were, what they looked like, who was their mother. My dad would tell me what he wanted me to know. I could always tell that there might be more to the story though.

My dad had always told me about his set of twins Martis and Vertis, and his next oldest, named Mario. Of course I knew about Jesse Jr., Tammy, Kelly, and then Timothy. Then he also had four children, including myself, in the Bay Area. That made a total of eleven children. I was always excited about how deep we were, even though I hadn't met the twins, or Mario yet.

One day when I was seven years old, after a long walk home from school, I had just hit the corner of my block leading to my house, when I saw my dad and two young men, older teenagers, standing in our driveway talking to one another. As I approached the driveway, I could hear my dad begin to introduce me to them, so by the time I walked closer, I could shake their hands and give them dap. They were two cool dudes, the type you would see in a teen flick. They were very athletic looking and just by looks alone, I could tell they were popular at school. The two guys had smiles on their faces as they dapped me up, and introduced themselves. The taller one was Clarence. The shorter one was Cory. My brother Justin had just walked outside too; he'd gotten out of school early because he was in kindergarten and they only had half days. He liked to watch Barney The Dinosaur back then, so that's what he was doing inside until he heard me walking up.

Once Justin got outside things got lively between us all. Cory and Clarence began to teach us some martial arts moves. They were expert martial artists and at such a young age, they were very fast, strong, and limber; real life warriors. Justin and I were super juiced! We were learning advanced moves and just knew we were doing something! With our dad looking on in approval, Justin and I kept at it. Cory and Clarence made sure that we had the techniques they just showed us down pat, then they went back to chat with my dad. After a little while they both said their "see ya laters" and left. My dad informed us later that day that he would be opening up a martial arts school and that Cory and Clarence would be helping him teach, Justin and I were through the roof with excitement. That entire week while I was at school, my dad, Cory, Clarence, and Justin would drive to Oakland Chinatown to purchase weapons and martial arts supplies. I'd arrive home daily to new gear stacked in my dads van.

At this time in my life, our home was still looking pretty cool inside. There were a few unpacked boxes that had been ignored, but for the most part, everything appeared to be in order. My mom was experiencing the pain of what had happened while giving birth to my little sister, however, at that time, it seemed like she was simply enduring the post-birth healing process that women face after having a child. The clutter, squalor, and hoarding hadn't quite manifested yet.

When my dad finally opened the dojo, Cory and Clarence were right there to assist him. Cory is a master artist as well, and he was the one who painted the company name and the dragon mural on our dojo window. He actually had to paint the mural twice because the first time he illustrated the Mortal Kombat dragon on the window, which was a huge copyright violation. Once he painted the new mural, it was actually better than the first one.

The fight school opened up to much acclaim, and many parents brought their children by to sign up for classes. Cory and Clarence became instructors, and we're probably the youngest black belt instructors in the entire city. During the day time private lessons would be held, and during the evening group lessons would be instituted.

As they got more comfortable with the layout and arrangement of things, Cory and Clarence would invite there teenaged peers over during the daytime to kick it at the dojo. They had just graduated high school so what better place than a dojo to kick it. Pun intended. As stated earlier, they were very popular, especially with the girls. They'd be on the office phone all of the time, "talking to chicks" and making plans. My mom used to complain to my dad, telling him that he shouldn't be having those young men "calling long distance and running his telephone bill up like that." He always just shrugged it off.

During this time in pop culture, the video game frenzy was really taking off. Nintendo and Sega were neck to neck in sales. It was Mario & Luigi versus Sonic the Hedgehog and Tails the Fox. My brother Justin and I really wanted a Sega Genesis video game console, but my mom and dad said "no, it's too expensive." I remember what appeared to be a quite request made from Cory to my dad about my dad purchasing Cory a Sega Genesis. I thought it was kind of a strange request, seeing how my brother and I had asked for one of those gaming systems and was shrugged off. Cory's request seemed validated though because it was presented as a payment for instructing martial arts classes if I remember correctly. Cory eventually got the Sega Genesis gaming console and a copy of the hottest game at the time: Mortal Kombat.

He let us play the game every once in a while, but for the most part, kept it with him at the dojo for whenever he and his friends got together. I was like "huh?" but went with the flow because I thought it was a payment he deserved for instructing at the school. Justin and I did have a regular Nintendo with a copy of Duck Hunt and Super Mario Bros. though. Cory taught us all of the glitchy tricks that were hidden in that game, so we were satisfied with what we had at the end of the day. The dopest trick he taught us on Super Mario Bros. was how to get infinite lives by stomping on a turtle shell in a certain place in World 2. You couldn't tell us nothing!

By this time I really grew respect for Cory and Clarence, so I began to refer to them as brother, and they would refer to me as their little bro. Cory would give me art advice and Clarence would give sound wisdom whenever he felt it appropriate. Clarence had always been into acting and script writing, so he often found himself on some marital arts movie set of the 1990's. He made some pretty cool connections over the years. They both furthered their martial arts acumen together, reaching high ranks in many styles.

As time went on, they would eventually join the military. That was shocking to me, but as an adult now, I can tell they just wanted to make the best of their young lives while they still could. Cory joined the Army and Clarence joined the Marine Corp. My dad was a Marine and would make fun of anyone who wasn't, so when Cory joined the Army my dad gave him a healthy dose of jokes and ridicule. All three of them, my dad, Cory, and Clarence, had gotten pretty close and I figured that he was a mentor of sorts to them. They began calling him "dad" and I thought it was a term of endearment. When they enlisted into the military, they had both stated how much the wanted to follow in "dad's footsteps". I took it as a sign of respect and felt thrilled to have two "play brothers" that I respected greatly as well.

When they left for boot camp and basic training, things got a little quite for a while. My dad had closed the dojo permanently and was focused more on his private security company that he'd been running simultaneously. This is also the time when my moms flare ups really began, and things around the home became more intensive. Her temper with me really shortened. So much so that when I was sent to my dad by her in frustration, all he'd say is "son, do what ya mama asked you to do and keep the monkey off your back." You wanna talk about "fatherly wisdom"; sheesh. That "monkey" was more like "King Kong" let me tell you!

Much time came and went. By now, my parents were back together, and my mom was feeling way better. They had even purchased a new home together and had been living in it for a few months. The year was 2020, June 20th to be exact, during the beginning of the "plandemic", when I got a text from my mom. She said "Jooge, your dad just told me something that has blown my mind!" It was my wife and I's wedding anniversary so I was focused on what we were doing, but casually texted my mom back and asked what she was referring to. She told me "your father just revealed to me that Cory and Clarence are his sons, and that Cory's sister Brenda is his daughter, and that Clarence has a twin sister named Claraissa who is his daughter too." I was like "whoaaa slow down, pump ya breaks!" I didn't even know that Cory had a sister and that Clarence was a twin! I especially didn't know that they were my real brothers! You mean to tell me this entire time I had been around two of my actual brothers and didn't even know it?! My mom told me that my dad said "I knew", but I really didn't know. I consider myself to be the family genealogist so when I found this news out, I kind of flipped. It was great news to receive, it was just a little mind-blowing. Everything began to make sense. Cory and Clarence being allowed to do what they'd do at the dojo with friends. Cory getting the Sega Genesis game console. Both of them joining the military to "be like dad". He wasn't just a mentor to them this entire time, he was their actual father!

This was the beginning of even more revelations to come.

2021 hit, and my eldest sister Tammy passed away. About a day or so after I had found out, my sister Brittany texted me saying how this "young lady was looking for her family, and thinks we are her siblings." I was like "ok, send me her IG profile and I will reach out to her." She sent it to me and logged into IG to see who this young lady was. As soon as I saw this young lady, I knew immediately that she was my sister; I mean immediately. I dm'ed her and within five minutes were chatting on the phone. She mentioned to me how she was born and raised in the Bay Area, like myself, but was raised in West Oakland.

We immediately hit it off.

Her father, or the man she thought was her father had passed away when she was four years old, and her mother had passed away soon after her eighteenth birthday. She had it rough in life too but wasn't a complainer and I we could relate to one another.

Before reaching out to Brittany, she had taken an Ancestry DNA test, the results of which led her to get in contact with Brittany. Her and Brittany shared DNA percentage was extremely high, so I knew she was definitely closely related once I saw a screenshot of her results compared with Brittany's results. Now it was all about finding out if she was a long-lost niece, or actually my sister. What made things even crazier is that her and I were both born in 1985, and she was a few months older than me.

I ordered us a sibling DNA test and once it arrived, Brittany and I drove out to visit the young lady in person for the first time. We took the sibling DNA test and I had the specimens expedited for quick processing. We agreed that I wouldn't open the emailed results once they arrived, and that I'd drive back out to her house and we'd review them together. The results arrived quickly and I made due on my promise. I drove with Brittany back out to the young lady's house and I opened the results with them standing in front of me. "Drum-roll please!", is what I proclaimed. The DNA results read "we are happy to inform you that we received your specimens for testing and that results indicate you are 99.9999% a sibling match."

Wow. I knew it! We knew it! What a blessing this news was! We jumped for joy! I had me a new sister and was so excited. Debra is her name.

I had always asked my mom if "I was a twin" throughout much of my early life. Occasionally I would ask her as I got older, but she would just look at me like I was crazy. Due to the fact Debra and I were born the same year we began referring to each other as "twin".

As soon as we settled down, Brittany pulled out her phone and opened Ancestry. Now that we knew what DNA percentages looked like in correlation to siblings, we applied our focus to another individual who had popped up in her close results. Come to find out, we had another sister, born two years after Debra and I, in 1987. Her name is Joelle.

By the time the year 2022 hit, another set of twins was revealed. They were born in the early eighties before my dad moved to the Bay Area. Their names are LaVon and JaVon.

Now, the total number of accounted for children my dad had bumped up from eleven to nineteen. I'm honestly just sitting back at this point, waiting to see how many more "sibling surprises" I receive.

Throughout life, some of us know how many siblings we have, and some of us not so much, even when we thought we did know. Others have always believed they were the "only child" to find out later that they are part of a larger family that they had no idea they'd be members of.

I personally love each and every sibling I've been blessed with. Relationships can obviously be complex when everyone isn't raised in the same household, let alone finding out about each other later in life. Each birth was Divine and

Blessed. We are all gifted with talent in our own respects. I hope that we can all heal from the trauma of how we arrived onto this earth realm and how we've been able to navigate since.

7

"Infighting. Gaslighting. Truth Hiding."

As a child, and teenager, I suffered an extreme case of gaslighting abuse, the effects of which followed me throughout my young adult life, causing me to doubt myself from deep within for a very long time. I didn't realize what I was experiencing, nor was I aware that what I'd experienced had a medical term associated with it.

According to an article issued by the *Newport Institute* on November 4, 2021, gaslighting "is a form of psychological manipulation in which the abuser attempts to sow self-doubt and confusion in their victim's mind. Typically, gaslighters are seeking to gain power and control over the other person, by **distorting reality and forcing them to question their own judgment and intuition**."

I was always under the impression that my gifts and talents weren't developed enough for the individuals closest to me to assist me in getting to the next level of my journey. I had always thought "they're just hating on me" or "they are just waiting for me to make it big before they begin celebrating my successes". I had no idea that the individuals in my life were psychologically manipulative and were seeking to sway the way I thought in order to control a potential narrative that I'd realize within myself; one that needed to be shared with people who could assist me in the healing process some day. A narrative that might "out" their horrible treatment of me, and shed light on the experiences I encountered while under their care.

For the longest time I'd create a narrative in my mind that sought to protect them. Knowing and remembering the truth is not an easy thing to cope with. Harboring so many concealed emotions, especially for as long a duration of time as I had, definitely affected me in ways I'm just now beginning to uncover and realize. I've always said: "uncovering the truth is like cutting into an onion. The more layers of truth you peel away, the more tears you will cry." I had a *James and The Giant Peach* sized onion before me. The emotional healing from such would be difficult, as well as intense.

I was blessed with the "memory of an elephant" is what I've always proclaimed. I was also blessed with a heart that remained warm throughout the coldest moments of my life. Replaying my past, over and over again in my head, began causing me to foster sympathy for my abusers. I didn't want them to "feel as bad as I had" even though they apparently never thought or felt the same regarding me. If they had felt the same as I, they never initiated those feelings with action.

Marshall Mathers, the multi-platinum recording artist also known as Eminem, was a huge influence on many children in my generation. He first hit the music scene while I was in the eighth grade. A young, quick-witted Rapper, Eminem's lyrics were a series of cutting-edge, "slap you in the face" written and recited forms of verbal therapy, which I can now identify in my adulthood as a clear cry for help. In those days of Rap music, there were many acts that I could identify with because they seemed to be witness to the same struggles I had experienced. Eminem had a very distinct style of writing and delivering his lyrics that honestly, made me quite nervous. In the Hood, we'd chalk his style up as "White Rap", meaning that Eminem was faced with personal issues that didn't quite resonate with us in the Hood, but due to his ability to flow like no one else on earth, we couldn't deny his ability to rap. He would often talk about his relationships with those closest to him, especially that of his mother and girlfriend. The songs would be gruesome and filled with malicious ideas and suggestions that definitely substantiated the exigency for the Parental Advisory labels placed onto all of his albums, hence the reasons for the nervousness I felt in regards to his music. Furthermore, it felt as though Eminem was using the genre of Rap and the Culture of Hip-Hop as his own personal psychiatric center. He needed to free himself from the truths and perspectives that he held deep within his mind.

People of Color had been marginalized within society for so long, that we didn't look at our private lives with each other as being psychologically toxic and emotionally draining. We've been the victims of so much externally based mental, physical, spiritual, and emotional trauma, that we seldom, if ever, recognized the internal strife also created and encountered from within. Someone had seemingly tipped Eminem off, that he wasn't experiencing life in the way that was most beneficial for him, and he wasn't happy about that. He found an outlet in the form of Rap Music, and he went all the way in with it, meaning that if he identified you as a target for a line of lyrics in one of his songs, he was going to talk about you until his conscience was cleared concerning you. I call this "The Eminem Approach" to healing and self-expression. After listening to an Eminem song, I'd wonder how the subjects of his sentiments had felt after they caught wind of his perspectives. I could never speak on my past situations in the same manner, could I? The issue with The Eminem Approach is that two wrongs don't make a right, they make a wrong wrong, and the future emotional turmoil Marshall clashed with internally once the songs and recordings were released globally, caused him another form of depression, stemming from the harmful effects of explicitly "outing" those whom he actually cared about the most in life.

I told myself early in my Rap career that I would avoid "The Eminem Approach" at all costs. If I could identify a balanced system that would allow me to identify my truest thoughts, and at the same time speak on my experiences so that I could heal from them, while also refraining from explicitness, I'd take it. I began rapping and producing my first beats when I was about fourteen years old.

I wrote my first rap when I was ten years old to the "I Got 5 On It" instrumental. "I Got 5 On It" was a huge hit originally penned by an East Oakland based Rap duo named The Luniz and a soul-singer by the name of Michael Marshall, that went on to see International success. I was also in the fifth grade at the time and had began learning how to write Haiku, an elaborate form of Japanese poetry focusing on precise thought and syllabification. The style helped me to see words differently, and I became really good at it.

I had always been a musician. For as long as I could remember I had been making some form of music. From beatboxing and drumming with my hands onto my thighs or onto a desk, to creating my own makeshift instruments, music was and still is close to my heart. It had always been an outlet for me. My own personal psychiatrist. The ability to capture my deeply hidden emotions and manifest them through the sounds of music, have definitely been one of my saving graces over the course of my life. I'm extremely grateful for music. While attending my elementary school, I wasn't allowed to join the band until I was in the fourth grade. Up until that point we'd been given recorders, an upright type of flute, to play. I already had some experience playing musical instruments by that time however. At the age of two years old I received a Playskool Saxophone and taught myself how to play "Twinkle-Twinkle Little Star". I carried that music notation and composition success with me everywhere I'd go.

Once I got to the fourth grade and wanted to play the saxophone, I was blocked by school protocol, and was unable to play it. Their reason was that I was "too young" and would have to wait until the next school year. In the meantime I'd be forced to play either the flute, clarinet, or the trumpet. To this day, I'm confused as to how the clarinet, another woodwind instrument like the saxophone, made it onto the "early learners" list, while the saxophone didn't, but okay, whatever. I chose the trumpet. Once I began conducting my due diligence on the trumpet, I realized that some great men had pioneered the instrument. I read about Dizzy Gillespie and Miles Davis. I also read about Louis Armstrong. It was Louis Armstrong that had the largest influence on me at the time. Miles Davis would become a major influence later in my life once I began producing music for myself, doing my best to keep the air of innovation and genre fusion within my musical approach.

When time came for me to get my trumpet, I met opposition from both of my parents. They hadn't had to invest in an instrument for me up to that point. They had been doing their best to avoid the topic of getting me a saxophone and were happy that the school wouldn't allow me to play it yet. When it was time to get my trumpet, they decided to rent me one from the local music store, instead of investing into one for me. Most of the children who played the trumpet, inherited theirs from either a father or a grandfather.

I wasn't allowed to go to the music store originally. My mom ended up going by herself while I was in school. When I returned home from a long day in class, thinking I'd have a trumpet waiting for me, what I actually saw was nothing like what I'd imagined. There on the couch, in a short, oddly shaped little case, laid an instrument I'd never seen before. I opened the oddly shaped case, and there inside, laid a cornet. A small, scraggly looking cornet. I was devastated. All I could say was "I don't know what this is, but it definitely ain't no trumpet!" My mom, going to the music store without me, brought home a cornet. I took it out of the case to show her. She didn't realize that what she had rented was not a trumpet. I placed the mouthpiece into the neck-hole of the instrument and began to play it. Not having played the trumpet or cornet up to that point, all I could muster up was a hard blow of air and the slight vibrations of what sounded like the beginnings of a horn being played. I asked her if we could please exchange it for the trumpet I'd been studying for. It was getting late and the music store closed earlier than most businesses, so I had to keep that horn overnight. The next day we went to the music store together and were able to exchange the cornet for the trumpet and a notation booklet to get me started with scale exercises. Even though it wasn't a saxophone, I was happy; at least it wasn't that dastardly cornet. No offense to all the cornet players of the world.

Band life was to prove itself a great season of my childhood that I enjoyed immensely. When it came to study of any sort, I truly only loved attending the mandatory weekly band practices. I'd reluctantly have to make sure I went to school, so that I'd be eligible for band rehearsals. Class was held at Vallejo Junior High-school.

The director was a stern, but fun man by the name of Mr. Whalp. He was a multi-instrumentalist who was very keen on the type of sound he wanted his band to produce. All of my band mates were bussed in from each elementary school in the district. We had a few students from one school, a couple from another school, and a handful from another. And so it went until all of the chairs were taken. We were a pretty musical bunch of children. I personally loved the experience. I was able to leave the elementary school, and travel every Wednesday to the junior high school for the day. I felt like a "big kid", and I loved the responsibility of being able to leave one school that catered to younger children, and join the ranks of the older children who got to leave class between periods, stand in line at the cafeteria, and pay for their own lunch. I loved being trusted with that level of dignity, and honestly, I despised having to return to my normal school at the conclusion of every day. I could definitely identify with Cinderella in that I was at my dream school doing what I loved, but once the clock struck 2pm I had to pack up my instrument and head back to the elementary school. I worked hard to earn my chair in Mr. Whalp's band; nothing was given freely and each student had to prove why they belonged within its prestigious ranks.

After working very hard and proving that I belonged in the band, I immediately earned First Chair of the horn section. To become First Chair in any section of the band is a great honor. You're the leader. You have to make sure that not only are you playing the musical selections correctly, but that your section mates are playing correctly too. You have to really develop an ear for the music. I loved every single moment of it. I remained a part of Mr. Whalps band for three years. When it was time to get promoted to the seventh grade and finally attend Junior High school, recruiters from each school in the district visited my elementary school to introduce us to what life might be like at each Junior High school. Naturally, I wanted to attend Vallejo Junior High school where Mr. Whalp would continue being my band teacher. My mother had other ideas. She was adamant against me attending VJHS and instead enrolled across town at Springstown Junior High school; I was totally crushed. For the first time since I began elementary school, I wouldn't be attending the same school as all of the friends I had grown with up to that point. I didn't have a report with my new band teacher, nor was I exactly familiar with the day to day system at Springstown. It seemed like every time I got into the groove of something I loved, it was taken away from me.

My mom and I had serious strains in our relationship at this point. Our infighting actually took hold full-fledged by the time I reached the third grade. I was eight years old and just trying to survive. Her injury was not being managed properly and she always got frustrated with me quickly and yelled at me often, especially if I was unable to immediately grasp a concept she was trying to get me to understand. I was frustrated because the house was growing dirtier and dirtier by the day. I didn't have the picturesque environment that I felt I should have as a child being required to learn new concepts. She blamed my lack of attention on me, instead of realizing that our home environment wasn't conducive to anyone learning educational concepts or completing homework. I was in between a rock and a hard place; well, more like papers, junk, and unused items and a hard place.

I seemed to be the main target of her aggression.

This is why I was so confused whenever she showed up to the Parent-Teacher meetings acting like her and my father actually cared about the grades I received in school. This is also why I was so confused when she would attend

PTA and School Board meetings under the auspice of assisting other parents and students with the kind, and nurturing aspects of herself that I'd desired from her at home. She would literally stand in front of an entire school advisory board and make it seem as though her house was in order, and that I was just a stubborn little boy who didn't want to do his homework and school assignments. I literally had little to no motivation to do any of the work given to me by my teachers. All I could think of is, "I'm being raised by a Cal Berkeley graduate, if this is what I have to look forward to after going through all of this 'schooling', I'm good, no thank you!"

As I grew older, I realized that there might be something wrong with my moms mental state of being. However, I wouldn't be able to confirm this notion until I got older and had a family of my own. I need you to understand; she had the capacity to complete the highest levels of academia, very book smart in her own right, and yet, when it came to her relationships with her children, she'd pick and choose which ones she wanted to cultivate and which ones she'd allow to wither. I think the biggest "mind game" (I want to use the "f-word" instead of 'game') of all is when she would do something for me that appeared to be kind. I had to learn that some people only do kind things for others to ease the burden of guilt they may have accumulated over a period of time; not really focusing on the victim's well being, but using the random act of kindness to abdicate themselves of any wrongdoing.

As I child who had to experience this type of behavior from a parent, it can be not only confusing, but disastrous in the child's well-being and mental health. The child will always assume and feel that they are never quite "good enough" at anything they do in life. When a parent repeatedly denies or disputes your unique experiences and feelings as being false or contrived, causing you to question your own intuitive abilities, you begin to doubt your experiences, and you begin to feel bad about yourself. Even worse, when a parent places blame on the child and relinquishes responsibility of any wrongdoing on their part, and blames the child for the conditions experienced, not only is that a form of gaslighting abuse, but it is downright cruel and unusual punishment.

It took me many years to reach the point where I began to trust myself and my own intuitive abilities again. Those intuitive abilities never left me, instead they laid dormant, only surfacing when I truly needed them, but because I hadn't had the chance to openly utilize and confirm them, I didn't recognize them for quite some time.

I moved through life floating for quite some time. All I knew was that I wanted to be a good person. I knew that whatever I had gone through, I didn't want anyone else to have to endure it; I wanted it to stop with me. By the grace of the Most High Mama & Papa I was able to maintain a deep sense of innocence. I actually thought that there was something wrong with me. I didn't even know I was the "black sheep" of the family. I just thought that everyone else had their own "stuff" to deal with and couldn't make the time to notice me. I was confused as to how I could genuinely love them and their "stuff", but they could turn a cold-shoulder to me. Those were some pretty rough days.

I'm so thankful to have made it this far. I do not take my life for granted. Now, I'm expecting them to read this book, make the necessary adjustments, and implement the changes I've mentioned. I'm also expecting them to keep a mask on and act like 1. I'm crazy and making this whole narrative up, or 2. Act like they've never been in favor of any of the issues I highlighted in this book and continue to push my truth to the side as though it's all been contrived.

There were many moments where I've held back in telling my complete story because, as I continually state, this book isn't about victim-hood, and it's not about making the perpetrators feel like crap. It's a book about accountability and taking charge of our lives once we have the ability and recognition to do so. This book is about healing and gratitude. This book is about being able to take what's happened over the course of my life on the proverbial chin and continue fighting another day. This book is a reminder to be thankful in all aspects of life, enjoying the Divine Refinement Process as much as humanly possible. I've gone from a tarnished metal to burnished gold. I've learned the process of alchemy by living through and undergoing the day to day travail, and operation, of such an endeavor.

Thank you to everyone who played a role in shaping and molding me into the Divine God Man I am today. I am a Reflection of the Divine. I am a Son of the Most High Mama & Papa.

A lion and lioness has a baby lion.

A hippopotamus and a hippopotamus have a baby hippopotamus.

An eagle and an eagle have a baby eagle.

A God and a Goddess have a baby God or Goddess.

I was made in the Image of the Most High Mama & Papa, therefore I Am...

Their child.

Just like the journey of manhood isn't predicated upon a destination; "I pay the bills, so now I'm a man", but instead, is an ongoing process of self-refinement and introspection. The journey of self-discovery is not predicated upon a destination, but a long drawn-out process, which only the very blessed can count themselves worthy of attaining.

What a blessing this wonderful adventure called life is!

8

"Gratitude. Gratitude. Gratitude."

"**14** What then shall we say? Is God unjust? Not at all! **15** For He says to Moses, "I will have mercy on whom I have mercy, and I will have compassion on whom I have compassion." **16** It does not, therefore, depend on human desire or effort, but on God's mercy. **17** For Scripture says to Pharaoh: "I raised you up for this very purpose, that I might display my power in you and that my name might be proclaimed in all the earth."
18 Therefore God has mercy on whom He wants to have mercy, and He hardens whom He wants to harden."
   -Romans 9:14-18

Many of us deal with our life experiences from a perspective of lack, which eventually leads us to complain about what we've been through or don't have, instead of counting the many blessings we do have. We are blessed to have experienced all that we have because each experience was an intrinsic element to our growth and character development.

I feel that I must continue to remind you: this narrative that I am sharing with you is not one of victim-hood, but one of overcoming necessary obstacles in order to achieve the greatest soul refinement possible while existing within this physical realm.

I quoted the Scripture above, to help illustrate my parents role in my life. How you view them after reading my story matters to me. Not so much for their sake, but for your own. I hope that you haven't grown angry or upset at them on my behalf. How I view them after the completion of my story matters to me as well. I have replayed many of the scenes shared within this book, over and over again in my mind. There were moments when I did not know why I was experiencing what I had to experience.

What matters to me most in regards to my earth parents is that, now that those major roles are completed in their lives in regards to our experiences together, will they too be able to "step off stage", and truthfully reflect on the roles they played? Will they be able to decompress, or will they remain within the burden of a role, located on a page of the script, that has long been turned? Will they remain on stage long after the curtain has been closed? This is why the scriptures say that God:

"has mercy on whom He wants to have mercy, and He hardens whom He wants to harden."

You, my earth parents, as well as myself, have roles to uphold in this Cosmic Play we've all been called to perform in. For me to harbor resentment, animosity, and anger towards them, is to harbor resentment, anger, and animosity towards myself. If we all would learn how to express ourselves from a perspective of enlightenment, one of the first things we'd realize is that we have all been given the opportunity to tell one heck of a story! I'm not the only one who has had traumatic experiences in life. I am one of the ones who has done his best to make sense of what has taken place throughout his life, but I am not the only one. Nor is my story comprised of the absolute worst experiences one can face.

Some individuals face traumatic experiences in a matter of moments, come and gone within the time-frame of ten minutes. The effects of those moments, which seem to be quick in how they happened, can last an entire lifetime though. For the most part, my experiences weren't comprised of quick moments, but were more akin to a chronic debilitating illness, lasting the span of many seasons. The experiences of both individuals, however intense, are valid and stand on their own, not to be compared to each as one being more intense than the other. Instead, those experiences should be viewed as experiences catered to each individual which were necessary for the physical, mental, and spiritual growth of the one who experienced it. In this way, we can share our stories of experience, not from a "woe is me" perspective, but from a perspective of true introspection, and eventual healing. When we have sympathy for ourselves, we can begin to recognize the value of having sympathy for those who were intrinsically involved in our growth. In fairness, many of us are unaware of the refinement process while we are smack dab in the middle of it. This is where the majority of our pain and need for pity derives from. If we were made aware of the Golden outcomes we'd eventually experience, we'd probably be more interested in the actual process it takes to arrive at that Golden place in life. Wisdom tells me that many of us still wouldn't appreciate the process however, due to a little something called "free will".

Procrastination is an actual thing. If people were made aware of the outcome before it manifested, they more than likely would not participate in the process to get there. We've always lived in a world where people sought to receive value with as little amount of energy expended as possible. The term "work smarter, not harder" comes to mind. The refinement of a tarnished soul into that of a Golden one, is a difficult process indeed!

The following sections of this chapter will be dedicated to true healing and gratitude. Learning how to accept what has happened to us as belonging to the conglomeration of actualized experiences manifested within the Great Cosmic Play is one of the most important aspects of perception and perspective we can be blessed with. It is of my deepest intent that true healing and gratitude be realized for us all.

Parents

Were they present in your life?

- If yes, be as grateful as possible that they did their best to be there for you.
- If no, think deeply about the people or person who *was* there for you. Be grateful that they stood in for those who you thought should've been there.

We all tend to create the "The Perfect Scenario" in our minds, and when that "perfection" isn't met, we become resentful and ungrateful. That "Perfect Scenario" is often influenced by the experiences we witness others being blessed with, instead of counting our own experiences as the blessed moments allotted to us.

- There are people who genuinely wish they were orphans because they have a strained relationship with their parents.

This mentality takes root because these individuals weren't taught how to love themselves; the person they see in the mirror. We are the one housed inside the physical avatars that we see in the reflection. Many still don't know and realize this. They must learn how to be grateful for their lives by recognizing that their own uniqueness is The Gift our world needs.

- Then, there are people who genuinely wish that they had an earth mother and father in any capacity because they are orphans, or didn't have biological parents they could depend on daily.

Due to circumstances outside of their control, some people have to endure a level of experiences that guides them to trust others who would normally appear to not have any interest in them. What I find most assuring is that The Most High Mama & Papa always sends some loving soul to step into that role of parental figure.

Material Wealth
Having vs. Not Having -
Everyone "receives" something. Forget about the "quality" of the things for a moment.

- Jordan Brand shoes cost $16.25 to make in the factory.
- The Apple iPhone 13 costs $570 to make in the factory.

Both of these items cost substantially less to manufacture than their retail price. Once branded, they become too expensive for the people who actually produce them to afford them.

The Catch
When you see how something is manufactured and produced behind the scene, knowing it's actual cost and inner workings, you'd more than likely laugh at those who pay extreme amounts for the item. It's all perspective.

Create Abundance Through Thankfulness
Write down everything that brings you joy in life.

Write down everything that makes you happy.

- Don't focus on how you obtained a thing. Just record it and write in thanks that you received it.
- Later on, you can focus on how you got it.

As you review your list, begin to think about how received what you got. Who gave it to you?

- Who provided you the opportunity to work for or receive what you have?
- Now write them down. Be thankful for them and their place in your life.

Continued to do this, a little at a time.
   Your list will grow and grow.

You will begin to notice how truly abundant you are.

You will soon realize that you were better off for anything not on your list. That it would be best that you did without it.

Many of the things that we think we want in life will be the cause of true pain and unnecessary problems.

When we finally realize that our unique experience is catered to who we are in our deepest aspects, we can be thankful for all things done for and given to us.

Protect Yourself
   Protect your energy and newly realized gratitude by:

- Giving to the needy and less fortunate.
- And by sharing your unique gifts and talents freely with the world.

Implementation of these activities helps us to remain in gratitude and abundance because: how could we give so much, so freely, if we weren't abundant and grateful for what we have?

Mantras

- *"Thank You For The Wisdom To Be Grateful And The Gratitude For Being Wise."*

- *"Thank You My Divine Most High Mama & Papa For YOUR WISDOM WITHIN ME"*

My Words of Affirmation

- I Am Abundant (Asé)

- I Am Bountiful (Asé)

- I Am Kind (Asé)

- I Am Wealthy (Asé)

- I Am Giving (Asé)

- I Receive Freely, I Give Freely (Asé)

- Goodness Flows Through Me, And Goodness Flows To Me (Asé)

- I Bless Everyone I Meet, And Everyone I Meet Blesses Me (Asé)

- I Am Thankful For My Life (Asé)

- I Am Grateful For My Being (Asé)

- I Am Compassionate (Asé)

- I Am Love (Asé)

Thank You Most High Mama & Papa For These Words of Encouragement and Affirmation. Asé Asé Asé

A Prayer Of Gratitude And Thanksgiving

For this prayer to work (from my experience) you will need to recognize The

Most High Mama & Papa as One. Whenever you say "Mama & Papa" your heart should be extending to The Most High..

Prayer of Gratitude and Thanksgiving:

I thank you for this day and all you've done for me up to this moment, and I thank you for all that you intend to do for me.

May I always be accepting of your Divine Will in my life.

I accept what has happened to me, in the course of my life, as a part of my unique experience.

I thank you for blessing me with the strength to make it this far in the journey.

I am grateful for your presence in my life.

I am grateful for the abundance you've blessed to me.

I am grateful for the prosperity you've allotted to me.

I am grateful for being wise. And I thank you for making me wise to recognize the gratitude within.

Please continue to guide me according to your Divine Will over my life, and may I look forward to your Divine Will over my life always. It is perfect and just in all its ways.

Thank you Most High Mama & Papa.

Asé Asé Asé!!!

Finally

Revisit and reread these methods as you need to, growing with each activity as you carefully implement the techniques listed. Don't be afraid to speak these techniques out loud.

Now, you, I, and we, can live in **true healing and gratitude!**

Asé Asé Asé

9

"The Realization & Moral of the Experience"

"*The earth and who we are as humans is one huge performance stage where we are all serving as the living camera system for the Creatoress/Creator of this universe.*"

Hmm, which of these statements was more revolutionary: that we humans are avatars for a Being infinitely more powerful than us, or that this Infinitely Great Power was referred to in a balanced state of being as both Creatoress and Creator?

We are living in these physical bodies, aka avatars, and are each assigned the task to experience this physical realm on behalf of the Divine Spark within us. The Divine Spark is an infinite form of energy that finds its source coming from the Divine Fire, that same "consuming Fire" spoken of within the Bible.

Each of our avatars (our physical bodies) contains a Divine Spark within it. We here on earth simply provide access of the physical realm to the Divine Fire, so that It might be One with It's Creation. This is why religious and spiritual systems all across the earth claim that "God" is omnipresent; if It is housed within 7.8 billion people, and flows through every single thing created, then it should be immediately clear that there are always a pair of "eyes and ears" open to observation.

When we include the vast array of animal and plant life, along with inanimate objects like stones, clouds, and the wind…the idea of something being omnipresent takes on a whole new meaning.

I never wanted pity, that's why I always kept this story to myself.

I only share it at this precise moment in my life, to help another Soul realize that they too were magnificently created, and that they too will be delivered out of the traumas that they had to endure. To be tried in the Fire of Life, and refined from tarnished metal into gloriously burnished gold, is a blessing that only a few truly obtain.

Count yourself amongst the worthy Dear One.

We choose our destiny before incarnating to this realm we call Earth.

We are made to forget our mission, destiny and purpose in order to be fully submerged in the multiple experiences we will have, which will eventually reveal our purpose, and set us on our mission.

We manifest our own realities.

Once we graduate from one experience, we are moved on to another, which many times, will contrast the previous one; this is how we know that we have graduated.

These experiences are meant to serve as character building and training exercises for your ultimate purpose and mission while on this earth, in your present lifetime. It is also of my understanding that our present life's experiences were chosen based on the experiences of the previous life experiences we were blessed to go through. We are talking about the journey of the soul being refined and made perfect over many lifetimes, in order that it might attain its blissful and final state of perfection.

Proof of each one of these realizations I've just shared with you, as occurring in my life is that, while as a child living in the middle of the "hood" with no apparent way out, I was forced to live in total squalor. I thought my life would always be experienced from such conditions.

This was a secret that I felt I had to guard with all of my being. It was a burden that no child should have to bear. However, that is my earthly opinion. The facts of life in truth, are that I *had* to go through each and every obstacle I faced in order to become the One I am today. It *all* had to happen. Due to these obstacles and the conditions I faced, it is though my childhood had been drawn out longer than most people's. I finally made it to twenty-one years old, but was I really a man? Thirty-two years of my life were spent in the Hood. Thirty-two years. I have friends who never made it past thirteen years.

Whenever my mom would leave, especially out of town for any extended period of time, we would immediately begin to clean the house to the best of our ability. We'd begin throwing away this and throwing away that, but to no avail, as soon as she'd return, the inside of our home would also eventually return back to its previous state of squalor. It was very easy to blame her for the condition of the home because we felt that we made an effort to restore it to some sort of cleanliness. This is why it was difficult for me to accept that I could've possibly manifested that reality for myself; I never wanted to live within those types of conditions, but they were necessary for my growth in this realm. It took me a while to realize that not only had I manifested that particular reality, but each member of my family in that season of our lives, had also manifested that reality; it was a collective manifestation!

I take these early experiences as proof that we actually do choose our families before incarnating to this realm, and that each of us will undergo unique experiences with each other, until we separate and no longer share in those experiences collectively.

I passionately state this again: This story is not about victim-hood or pointing a finger of blame, it is about acceptance for what was, because each experience was tailor-made for me in order to strengthen my character and build me into the man fit to live within my predetermined destiny. I thought my parents, who'd been together my entire life up to the time I was fifteen years old, would now be separated indefinitely, and like so many others, I'd have to live in a reality with divorced parents. What eventually happened was quite the opposite.

Once I graduated from being surrounded by garbage, living inside a hoarding house, and was essentially removed from that experience, my parents eventually got back together, and began living the type of life that I thought we'd all live together. My younger siblings were able to live with them, never having to feel the pressure of being pushed out of my parents home. They now live in a sprawling home with many rooms that they always keep clean, a beautiful front and backyard with many healthy fruit trees and flourishing plants, and they even have the trampoline I always wished to have as a child! I was never allowed to experience that level of existence with them. Instead, I was driven to creates healthy and abundant environment for my own family, after years of hard work and dedication to the protection of my kindness, innocence, and warm, child-like heart. Whatever I had to endure, my children would not have to endure; the curse would be broken with me. If it wasn't a curse, but instead a marvelous blessing in disguise, they would learn the blessings lessons without having to endure any of the stressing. Either way, what began with me, would stop with me because I passed all of the testing required, along with the prerequisite's, in order to deliver one heck of a meaningful *testi*mony.

Today, my siblings are allowed to remain inside this new home as long as they want, while I'm the one who has never spent the night, nor have I been invited to spend the night. I have actually never stayed at their new home for longer than 3-4 hours at any given time. After carefully analyzing my journey, I began to realize that I was the common-denominator from my past into the present as it pertained to our relationship, and the experience we were all inundated with up to a certain point; once I was removed from their everyday life, they all changed and began living the life I originally thought was for *all* of us!

To say the least, this is where things get a little tricky.

Even though my younger siblings also experienced the same squalor as I did, their graduation eventually led them and our parents into the sprawling new home, the one we *always* thought we should be living in. When I graduated, I eventually purchased the sprawling new home that I always thought I should live in, and immediately moved my wife and children into it so that they could experience a lifestyle I'd never experienced fully until that point. We all finally graduated; my parents, siblings, and I. It may be difficult to accept, but it's true; we weren't victims after all. Instead, we each had lessons that we had to learn, where we were physically placed, in order to elevate to the next level of our existence here in this realm. We each had to remove the clutter from our minds and renew them. We had to essentially clear our minds of all debilitating debris, and change our thinking in order to receive the blessings we'd each always hoped for.

All of the players remained the same, the only one that completely exited the picture was myself. Could I really be as influential in manifesting my present reality as it seems? Am I really stronger and more powerful than I could've ever imagined?

As I've grown throughout the years and have received certain revelations, or "downloads" as we call them today, I've been made to realize that we humans are all to serve as the "eyes, ears, and vessels, of the Most High Mama & Papa".

What a responsibility that is!

When you really take the time to analyze this thought, and compare it to the current state of the world, one has to wonder: "The Most High is either the greatest fan of The Maury Show and loves more drama than one hundred Jerry Springer Show producers combined, or, we are so lost as a collective of people, that we've totally severed our connections to The Most High Mama & Papa, and they, sitting as One in the Heavenly Place, are shaking their head in absolute amazement at what we've forced them to witness day to day."It's almost like they are parents who went away on vacation, leaving the house to their adventurous but oftentimes unruly teenage children. You know, the type of parents who'd leave a list of rules and regulations, but also casually choose not to mention the recently installed secret security cameras strategically placed throughout the home so they could keep a close eye on things while gone to their vacation retreat. They know full well that their children aren't going to abide by the rules, but they test them in hopes that at least one of them maintains a sense of respect and responsibility. You and I both know how that story ends though: Somebody's definitely gonna be in trouble when Mama and Papa get home!

The Most High Mama & Papa; I sure do mention them a lot don't I? The reason is simple: they brought me through every single burden I've faced in this life and never once abandoned me. When my earth parents, the pro-creators of my earthly avatar, began to wild out, my Divine Heavenly Parents allowed me the opportunity to rise out of the quagmire of trauma and hostility, and into the rarefied air of greatness.

My prerogative is not to convince you of their existence, or to convert you into believing in them like some sort of missionary would. My job here is to carefully highlight aspects of my life that most individuals do not make it out of in one piece, or in one peace. There were many times that I wanted to give up. They would not allow me to though. They blessed me with so much hope and faith that everything would one day be okay.

I didn't realize just how much people were probably rooting for me until I met one of my aunties to assist her with some moving she was doing. It was a moment I'll never forget because it was the first time she "had me alone" without the lingering presence of her older sister, my mother, standing nearby. My auntie told me "I don't know how you got through it, but you did. I am so proud of you." She was referring to the toxicity I endured throughout my childhood into young adulthood. She was so thankful I'd "survived" and that she could still recognize Little Jujee. I was taken aback by her comment because I had always thought she was "ok" with the conditions we were living in. That was the first time I realized that maybe, just maybe, they saw my mom, or maybe both of my parents, as bullies that were living how they wanted to live and that one day each one of us children would either rise like a Phoenix from the ashes, or be consumed in the fire; either way, it wasn't "any of their business."

What had been revealed to me about the Most High Mama & Papa, is that they, together as One, were the Eternal Creatoress and Creator, the Source, of this entire Universe and everything contained within it. They stand outside of it, and within it at the same time. Their Eternal Essence flows intrinsically from the Divine Source of their Love, through the Universe non-stop. This thought is far from those taught to us within the realm of Christianity. It took many years of patience to finally be brought to this realization. Once I had arrived, the need to want to "spread the Gospel", the "Good News" wasn't on my heart at all. Instead I recognized the journey to that momentous realization as being my own, and that if someone else was going to form a similar realization as I, that they too would have to embark upon their own journey as well. A journey where only the strong survive and get to celebrate together at the finish line, not knowing that they weren't going to arrive alone.

I naturally love to share. What I love to share with people the most are good and hearty things. Things that make people smile, recognizing, realizing, and remembering the greatness within themselves. I don't like sharing in an attempt to make others feel like they aren't special, or that I'm the only one who is. I was a huge fan and supporter of "Show-and-Tell" while in elementary school. I've always liked the idea that the gifts and talents I've been blessed with could inspire and motivate others to find and utilize their own gifts and talents to do the same.

Without these avatars, vessels, vehicles, temples, aka bodies, we'd be invisible within this physical plane of existence. As avatars for the Eternal Spirit, we are constantly "streaming a live feed" back to the Most High Mama & Papa so that they can experience this 3D realm through us, from their Heavenly Placement; this is how they are omnipresent. They live through each and every one of us. We are much more than we have ever been told we are.

I've also never been one for coincidences. I genuinely feel that everything happens for a reason and that it is up to us to remain patient in waiting for the revelation of that reason if it is not immediately made known to us. Whenever something "good" happens to us we were "at the right place at the right time", but when something "bad" happens to us we were "in the wrong place at the wrong time." I never liked those statements. "Good" and "bad" are perceptions. Each perception changes with the one who perceived it. What's "good" to one, may be "bad" to another, and whats "bad" to one, may be "good" to another. It's my understanding that everything just "is". The saying "one mans trash is another mans treasure" comes to mind.

That everything just "is", is also a perspective in and of itself that most people don't share, which is okay too. That we are all at different points in our Soul's growth, is the awareness I'm seeking to highlight.

You are special. You are blessed and highly favored. You were led to this book for a Divine reason. You were incarnated to this earth realm for a Divine purpose. Please don't ever give up on yourself. If you only knew what the future held for your life.

Give thanks and show gratitude as often as you possibly can, each and every day.

Always remember that you are loved and appreciated and that someone has seen what you have gone through, and is cheering you on to success. You might not feel like it now, but you are a hero in the eyes of those who pray goodness over your life without ceasing.

Thank you Most High Mama & Papa for your Divine and Perfect Will being fulfilled in regards to our lives, always.

10

"What To Say, And How Not To Say It"

(So you don't say what you're not supposed to say)

Disclaimer - The information presented in this chapter is original, but in no way conclusive. However, great effort has been taken to ensure that the reader understands the concepts presented, and that new Statements of Desire can be correctly spoken and successfully implemented into your daily life. By the time you are done reading this chapter, you will absolutely know how to form and speak your own Statements of Desire, empowering your life forever more.

A Simple Guide To Speaking Blessings Into Your Life

The Law of Attraction is real. But, did you know that whenever we speak out loud, we attract the opposite of what we ask?

Even when we make a seemingly good statement, we aren't guaranteed to get a seemingly good result. We have been taught to speak entirely wrong. Likewise, we have been taught to vocally request those things we seek out of life entirely wrong; or have we?

When we speak correctly, we attract our deepest desires. When we speak incorrectly, we attract those things we we're trying to avoid.

Opposites attract. This is the first and only rule you have to commit to your memory if you intend to successfully incorporate the methods explained in this chapter.

Believe it or not, but when we speak positively, or at least the version of "positive speaking" that we've been taught, we actually magnetize negativity towards us. Remember, opposites attract, so when we make statements that appear to be positive, we are actually enabling the negative result to manifest in our subconscious mind.

In other words, when we make a statement of declaration for instance, our subconscious literally thinks of its opposite and begins to work on manifesting the opposite of what we ask for. Instead of the thing, or desired result of what we consciously ask for, we end up getting its opposite, which our powerful subconscious mind constantly developed behind the scenes!

Here is a list of some common statements that we would consider to be blessings. Upon taking a closer look, we can begin to identify the mistakes in these statements and rewrite them in a way that actually empowers us when we speak them.

If you want to take power over your life and begin to speak in a way that empowers your requests, please read the contents of this chapter carefully. As you continue to adjust your approach to how you speak, you will surely see a positive change to your life.

You will learn how **not** to speak your Statements of Desire, as well as learn the correct way that you should speak your Statements of Desire.

Let's use an example before we begin, so that we can get a clearer understanding of this method.

Death. To die. To leave the physical body.

Most people seek to avoid death, so we will use this energy thought-form as our example.

Normally, when a person seeks to live long, they will say, "I want to live forever!". Now, on the surface, this statement appears to be good. It appears to be correctly spoken because it identifies the desired result. Upon closer look however, you will soon learn that this statement is actually one of the worst statements you could ever make. Here's why.

The trick to speaking our desires into existence is to state the negative aspect, or detail, of the thing you don't want. Yes, you read that correctly. The subconscious will then begin to develop its positive, and just as powerful opposite. The difference here is that you actually desire the *positive opposite* that your subconscious will begin to manifest.

For instance, instead of saying:
   "I want to be healthy."

You should say:
   "I don't want to be sick."

You see what we just did? We stated the negative aspect, or detail, of the thing we don't want, in order to make subconscious space and generative energy for the aspect we do desire. To be healthy.

This chapter was written to help you see the truth about the words we speak. It is filled with examples of what not to say, followed by the correct manner in which to speak your desire.

You will begin to notice the verbal requests you make manifesting themselves in a positive manner. The more that you analyze and adjust your speaking habits, the clearer your intent to manifest your exact desires will be. To assist you in grasping this concept, each statement has been separated according to its correctness. Positive sounding, but incorrectly spoken Statements of Desire will be addressed first, followed secondly by the negative sounding, but correctly spoken Statements of Desire.

The successful implementation of these techniques will guide you to the life you've always thought possible for yourself.

Lastly, just so we are clear: each Power Statement, will be first introduced in its incorrect form, followed by the proper form in which it should be spoken.

Example
Instead of saying:
"I want to be healthy."

You should say:
"I don't want to be sick."

Again, do you see what just happened here?

When you spoke the statement "I want to be healthy" your subconscious mind began to activate. However, instead of your mind focusing on the immediate desired result of being healthy, it began to work on manifesting the opposite of the desired result which happens to be illness and sickness. The reason for this is due to the law of opposites attracting.

For this to make sense, all you have to do is think of a jigsaw puzzle.

To get to the desired result of an image sought to be manifested, a jigsaw puzzle-solver must identify which puzzle pieces correctly fit together. Jigsaw puzzles can be cut into simple shapes, or any number of several other alternative designations, but in order to fit together, there must be some give and take in each puzzle piece.

Speaking as a fully-qualified jigsaw puzzle solver myself, I can say that the standard word for a puzzle piece that was shaped and cut to feature a tab, is an "outie". The puzzle pieces with inward grooves are called "innie's". Most pieces have outie's and innie's, allowing for each piece to be connected.

Now that we have a basic understanding of how jigsaw puzzles work. Let's look at the deep insinuations behind this method of correctly speaking our desires into existence.

For the sake of this dialogue let's say that outie's are positive and that innie's are negative. With this understanding, we can immediately see that a puzzle piece designed to feature only outie's, will only fit with a piece that has at least one innie. It is the opposing design of the outie and innie that allow the puzzle pieces to connect, and form the image.

When our conscious and subconscious minds work together to form our manifested desire ("the image"), they operate similarly to how a jigsaw puzzle is put together. Space must be provided in order for a connection to be made. This is why when you speak a statement that appears to be positive, also known as a surface-level statement, it actually gives space for the negative aspect of itself to connect and manifest. The reason this is all made possible is because the negative aspect or counterpart of a desire, which is attached to the powerful subconscious mind where all of our manifestations derive from, has been activated to produce the result directed by the subconscious mind itself.

It must be stated that the reverse holds true, and is the motivation for writing this book, as well as serving as the impetus in delivering to you the proper way you should voice your desires. When you speak a statement that appears to be negative, also known as a surface-level statement, it actually gives space for the positive aspect of itself to connect and manifest.

Moving forward, this aspect is what we will be focusing on the most.

What Not To Say, And How To Say It

Here is a list of study words and phrases which will assist you in learning this simple, yet powerful technique of speaking your desires into reality. These are all examples that you can use. I suggest that you get the hang of them, paying attention to the slight nuances shown in each, and then practice them so that you can implement your own phrasing.

OBJECTS OF OUR DESIRE

- Happiness
- Success
- Joy
- Love
- Determination
- Achievement
- Friends & Social Life
- Marriage
- Hope
- Material Desires
- Personal Life
- Children
- Emotions
- Mantras

STATEMENTS OF DESIRE

HAPPINESS

Instead of saying: "I always want happiness in my life."
You should say: "I don't ever want a life filled with sadness."

SUCCESS

Instead of saying: "I will achieve great success."
You should say: "I will never be a failure in life."

JOY

Instead of saying: "I seek to live a life of joy."
You should say: "My life will not be one of misery."

LOVE

Instead of saying: "I will succeed in impressing my beloved."
You should say: "I won't be a failure in impressing my beloved."

DETERMINATION

Instead of saying: "I am going to keep on pushing forward no matter what."
You should say: "I will not let anything stop me along my journey."

ACHIEVEMENT

Instead of saying: "Whatever goals I set, I will achieve."
You should say: "I will not let any hindrances stop me from achieving my desires."

FRIENDS & SOCIAL LIFE

Instead of saying - "You will enjoy the company of good friends."
You should say - "You will despise the company of bad friends."
Suggested statement - "You will despise the company of bad friends."
Appearance - Surface-level, Negative.
Result - If you despise the company of bad friends, you create the space for your subconscious mind to connect your desire to manifest good friends. It is the Law of Attraction.

MARRIAGE

Instead of saying: "My marriage will be the best ever."

You should say: "I will keep my marriage from failing and crumbling apart."

HOPE
Instead of saying: "I am hopeful for a bright future."
You should say: "my future will not be dim and worthless."

MATERIAL DESIRES
Instead of saying: "In life I will have the best of everything."
You should say: "In this life I will avoid the worst of what life has to offer."

PERSONAL LIFE
Instead of saying: "I shall be happy and satisfied in my personal life."
You should say: "May I never be sad or unsatisfied with my personal life."

CHILDREN
Instead of saying: "I shall share a loving relation with my children."
You should say: "I will not have a hateful relationship with my children."

EMOTIONS
Instead of saying: "Peace and harmony shall prevail."
You should say: "Keep away from unnecessary arguments and stress."

MANTRAS
Instead of saying: "I am a light in the darkest of nights."
You should say: "The darkest of nights cannot overthrow my light."

The more you practice the techniques presented in this chapter, the more comfortable you will become with customizing these methods to suit your immediate needs. You will be able to successfully manifest anything, based upon your knowledge for rightly stating your desires. Continue to work on yourself and remember to be patient as you implement these phrases, as well as your own, into your daily speech patterns.

11

"Bringing Innovation Into Your Life"

T here is something about the word "innovation" that makes me excited, and feel the need for celebration. The reason for these feelings could quite possibly be rooted in the word itself:

"In - Ovation"

When we break the word up into its two key components, we see a great and welcoming surprise in that to be "innovative" one is "in ovation".

But "in ovation" of what exactly?

For starters, the innovator is in celebration, or "in ovation", for the ability to innovate!

It is this intrinsic ability to express gratitude through creating that the innovator establishes clarity of consciousness in order to move forward with the next phase of a project, or an entirely new project altogether.

Understanding this principle, how do we then bring innovation into our own lives? How do we reap the rewards of the thoughts we manifest into the physical realm?

The word "innovate" is defined as "making changes in something established, especially by introducing new methods, ideas, or products."

In this modern era we usually think of innovation as belonging solely to the **product design and manufacturing industry**. One of the reasons for this predicament is that we live in a capitalist society where there are new versions of old products introduced to the population constantly.

Product innovation is literally everywhere!

How then does an individual not be bombarded by the daily commotion of new product promotion, and focus on their own products, or maybe even something we'll call "self-innovation"?

The trick is to identify anything that inspires you and go after it.

Begin with your due diligence of the thing, making sure that it's something worthy of your pursuit. Once you've confirmed that your inspiration is genuine, you can begin to chisel away at all of the objectives that must be completed in order to make your goal a reality.

Elbert Hubbard, the profound writer and philosopher of the early twentieth century once said, "A little more persistence, a little more effort, and what seemed hopeless failure may turn into glorious success!"

As you begin to work and will your idea into reality, you will be frustrated. The frustration will stem from the outcome of an objective not matching up with the internal input of the initial idea. When this happens we must reevaluate our position.

This is the moment during the process where our ideas are tested and refined. During this process of creating, our ideas give way to further insight on how to deliver into the physical realm what we see in our minds. It is also during

139

these moments of reflection that innovation is birthed.

Keep in mind that there are moments where experience in a certain arena or industry give way to innovation as well. These moments aren't usually inspired by original foundational ideas, yet they serve a great purpose in delivering new methods and techniques because life in general continues to evolve and expand.

The key to bringing innovation into your life is identifying when you are feeling inspired. Wherever you find yourself to be the most emotionally involved is probably where you should begin to apply your focus on what, within that space, will inspire you to innovation.

Think about it. When a man meets a new woman he usually is not the first man she has ever dated or been with. This man, if he has any self-confidence, will identify the errors of the man who was with the woman before he was, and he will be emotionally inspired to innovate, and guide their current relationship away from anything the previous man did incorrectly.

Through his innovation, the new man will seek to erase the mental and spiritual energy applied by the man within the woman's previous relationship. This is one of the most primal of actions and is ironically often expected by the woman, even if it is not promoted as such. The reason for this level of non-promotion, or lack of vocality on the woman's part, is so that she can mete out who is actually interested in forming a relationship with her. If she openly promotes the qualities she seeks in a man, any man can falsely alter his character and have the woman believing that he is somebody that he truly is not. A man who is seriously pursuing a woman will naturally execute these characteristics in a healthy manner, establishing his presence in her life.

The idea of man pursuing woman is one that we all can relate to in some form or another.

Bringing Innovation into your life will also require an active awareness of what aspects of yourself you are willing to share with the world. The moment you take honest account of the personal gifts you are willing to share with the world, you will begin utilizing these gifts. Once you begin utilizing these gifts to assist and serve others, thru trial and error, innovation will make itself known to you.

As always, and in everything, give thanks and be grateful. Our ideas are gifted to us so that we might be of service to our fellow brothers and sisters while here in this earth realm, experiencing its intricacies together. Done correctly, innovation will empower you to leave a legacy to subsequent generations worthy of an ovation.

12

"Final Thoughts"

There were many great moments that I experienced early on. I've always done my best to be a "glass-half-full" kind of person. Due to this perspective on my life, I feel I was shielded or "blinded" to much of the trauma while I was living within it. I remember feeling like something wasn't "right" during many of the days of my upbringing, but then I'd go outside and play, and all of my friends helped me to ignore what was actually taking place inside my home.

Even though this book has been written to identify the traumas in life that one could experience, as well as how to navigate to a mental space of healthy healing, the moments that made me feel "good" or "okay" with those experiences, almost seem like checkpoints, or proverbial oasis's which were strategically placed or injected into my psyche in order to keep me moving forward to my eventual destiny. Each living day is our destiny fulfilled.

The good to great moments that made me happy or smile as a child, were also the source of great confusion to me. On the one hand, I truly did live, for many many years, in literal squalor, and I had to be totally silent about it. On the other hand, I had to act like I didn't live in total squalor, never wanting to expose my parents "nakedness" to those who could help remove me from those deplorable conditions. I was literally confused. It was this confusion that lingered within my mind for much of my young adult life as well, and what kept me from writing about my experiences. I was confused by my parents who sought to be professionals, an image they dispensed externally, but internally, they themselves required much healing. I was blessed to realize this early on. This is where my sympathies for them have always taken root.

I'm telling you, as I look back on my past with empathic eyes, I feel as though my parents did their absolute best to raise us, but there was clearly a spirit of delusion that had taken hold of them. As an adult myself now, I can see more clearly as to what was taking place back then. It took me arriving to adulthood and experiencing life as an "adult" to recognize what could've been going on way back then. I couldn't of fairly spoken on my traumatic childhood until I'd been consistently successful as an adult to identify what healthy behavior is versus what toxic behavior is.

Are any of us perfect? I emphatically say yes.

We are perfectly created and made to do all of those things, no matter the levels of comfortability of those things, in accordance with the greater destinies we are called to fulfill. We don't have to know the outcomes of the future, but we will live within each of our purposes, which will manifest that destiny into our realities. If we seek to learn from these moments, it's up to each of us to take self-accountability, recognizing our hand in them, and not dismiss the roles we play in bringing that destiny to fruition.

I don't want anyone to view my parents as if they were or are evil. That's not the reason or impetus behind the writing of this book. They were hurting internally as well. They were dealing unhealed childhood traumas as well. We trust our parents as children. If our parents mask what they've experienced in their lives, and don't seek healing for themselves, what begins to develop is a false sense of control and narcissistic behavior. That is what I was truly experiencing at the core of it all. Had my parents been forthcoming in their communication about the pasts that they endured through, I am positive that they could've healed, and we would've been protected from having to experience a similar situation ourselves, as their children. Even though we slept on the living room floor surrounded by clutter, my mom would tell us bedtime stories that she'd make up and share with us, calming our nerves after a long day in the world, helping us to also ignore what we were encountering within the four walls of our home as well. Even though we lived in tons of clutter, my dad still taught us how to say "Thank you Jesus" and would remind us to be thankful for the life we were given. We didn't know anything about the "real name of 'Jesus'" back then; my dad was doing his best to share what he knew. Even though learning about Yahushua's name matters in the long run, at the time, in those moments where we needed something or someone to believe in that was greater than ourselves, It didn't matter if "Jesus" isn't his real name; the energy behind the intent in saying "thank you" was always pure, just as Yahushua is. They both taught us how to pray for a better day and give thanks for the one we'd just walked through.

I'm convinced at this very instant that the entire experience was Divine and meant to take place; every single moment.

When I was sick, my mom and dad would worry. They would pray for my recovery. My mom would go to the grocery store and purchase items like ginger ale and soup that would heal me and make me feel better. My dad would go to Wendy's and purchase me a baked potato per my moms instructions, which she would then give to me in order see some energy restored to my bones.

On birthdays, up until a certain age, they would allow us to have little parties at Chuck E. Cheese or Scandia Family Fun Center, which we were always grateful for, even if afterwards we were to return home to our actual living conditions. It was like a scene out of Cinderella. Again, it was moments like these which really confused me. These moments also kept me from being spiteful towards them. Looking back, I can honestly say that I was protected from the anger towards them that I could've embraced as my eyes began to open in my adulthood. Instead, I've always felt sorry for them. I've always prayed for their internal healing. I couldn't understand why I'd gone through everything I'd been through, with them eventually living as if it were all "okay", ignoring my perspective and feelings, and ignoring opportunities to speak about the past in a non-toxic manner. I love to communicate and at times, even now, I feel that one of the greatest travesties encountered between us was the purposeful overlooking of the exigencies of a child to unpack his childhood traumas with the people responsible for his upbringing.

This book isn't about spite and bitterness. It's truly about one young mans experience through a series of seasons in his life, and how he was guided and protected along the way.

I will love my earth parents to life always.

They did everything they were supposed to do in order that I'd become the man I am today. Did they "know" what they were doing while in the moment? Maybe, maybe not. Were they used to influence me into a greater good and stature in my life? Most definitely.

When they see me today, I can tell I make them nervous. However, the question is: do I make them nervous because of the man I've become; that little boy who triumphantly attained manhood and who finally overcame all of the childhood trauma, or do I make them nervous because they know they've kept silent about my upbringing for so long, and that now that I'm an adult, I may do something like "write a book" and speak on those experiences publicly myself? Why did they refuse to take control of the narrative and guide me along the road of introspection as my earth parents, those ones seemingly responsible over me for so long? The short answer: it wasn't their job to. This is why I pray for them that their hearts will not be weighed down with carousing, drunkenness and the anxieties of life, as mentioned in the book of Luke chapter 21:34.

I've been derogatorily called "Moses", "Noah", "Israel", "Osama", "Abraham", and "Jesus", all in an attempt to ridicule the path I've been placed on and the journey I've been chosen for. I've had to transmute the energy of being derogatorily called those historical individuals into the good names and energy they were originally meant to inspire. I soon realized that calling me those names placed me in some good company, if that's who my image inspires them to think about when they see me. I give all the praise and credit to the Most High Mama & Papa for the strength I've been bestowed with, and I give them the eternal thanks for the tough plan and refinement process they placed me through in order to create in me the mind and heart that I have today. I love them to life always.

I have no complaints.

My hope is that instead of you, the reader, being upset about what I had to endure throughout my life (much of which I did not share within the pages of this book), that you can see the obstacles, not as barriers, but as the necessary spiritual mechanisms that would propel me into my greatness. My hope is that another young soul, who comes across the pages of this book, will be able to see my journey, resonate with it, and realize that they too can overcome the obstacles placed within their paths, without the weight of bitterness and spite weighing down their precious hearts, or clouding their minds into confusion and depression. It's not easy penning a book like this due to all of the settled emotions that must be stirred up again in order to bring them back to life. It's not easy to be at a place in life where these emotions have seemingly dissipated, only to return to the front of the mind to be remembered and spoken on, not to cause drama and strife, but to elicit deep thought and to possibly help another with their mental and spiritual healing while they encounter the obstacles of their journey in existence.

I hope you innerstand this.

You made it this far. Congratulations.

I know you will reach your destiny, so please, never give up. Tell your story. It's not my job to tell you how to tell your story. It's my job to provide you with a perspective on story telling that will enable you to retain your innocence and purity of heart, while sharing your experiences with the world. If you're willing to share it, I sincerely hope to read about it one day.
Be blessed in all that you do. Stay Vigilant.

I love you to life always.

- True Jus

www.ingramcontent.com/pod-product-compliance
Lightning Source LLC
Chambersburg PA
CBHW060528130626
46553CB00002B/682